Letters from Yemen

Letters from Yemen

No matter our age, we are all heroes of our own lives. Travel along with Jean Mondon, a 62-year-young English midwife as she recounts her two-year adventure of living and working for an NGO in the Arab Republic of Yemen in the 1980s.

Jean Mondon & Suzanne M. Elliott

ISBN-13: 9781983579554
ISBN-10: 1983579556

Suzanne Elliott
Santa Cruz, California
February 2018

Dedications and Thanks

This book is dedicated to my mother, Jean Mondon. Thank you for inspiring us to lead meaningful lives. You were the ultimate role model for strong women everywhere.

Thank you to my sister Katherine J. Mondon for copy-editing this book - you are amazing. Katherine is a professional copy-editor - thankfully for me. She can be contacted at email: katherine.mondon@which.net

Thank you to Barbara Oertli – professional graphic designer for designing the cover art for "Letters from Yemen" – Barbara may be reached at email: oertlidesign@yahoo.com

This book is a true story of what happened during the two years Jean Mondon lived and worked in North Yemen. Names of some of her co-workers/colleagues have been changed to protect their privacy. All other facts remain unchanged.

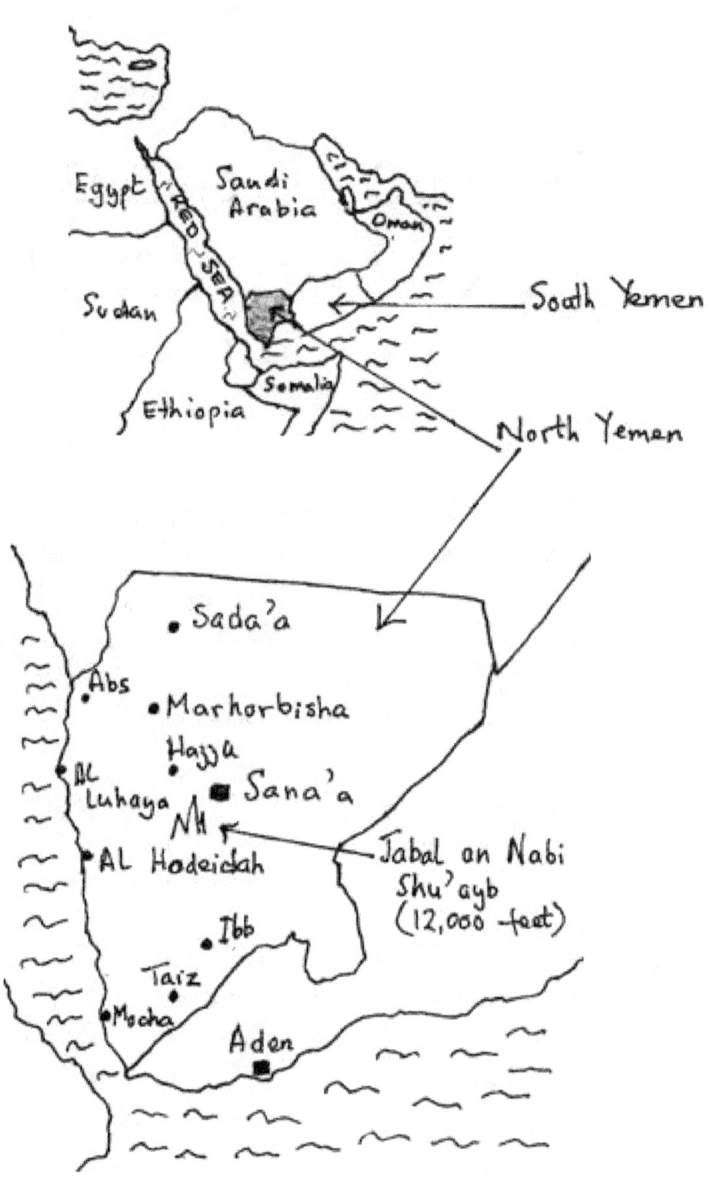

Map of North Yemen 1984

One

An Introduction to Jean Mondon

Written by her daughter, Suzanne Elliott (Mondon)

Jean Mondon was an extraordinary woman. I say this not because she was my mother but because it is true. She was born in 1921 on a small farm in the rural county of Shropshire in England. Her father was a tenant farmer and the family was always short of money. Children from such backgrounds could expect to receive only what was termed an 'elementary education'; usually this meant leaving school at fourteen and finding work. In Jean's case, she helped her parents in the home and on the farm. She was exactly eighteen when World War II broke out, and chose to become a nurse; this was one of the very few professions open to women with very little education at that time. She was trained in the county town of Shrewsbury and went on to Edinburgh to study midwifery. For her, nursing was likely to lead to an interesting and varied work life. In particular, it offered the chance to travel, something she had yearned for as a child.

After the war she signed up with the British Colonial Service to work in the small East African country of Nyasaland (now Malawi). Nyasaland was a British colony at the time and part of what was called the Federation of Rhodesia and Nyasaland. Jean sailed to South Africa on a troop ship and then traveled by train to Nyasaland. She went alone, but as a result of her early experiences there, several of her nursing girlfriends from Shropshire joined her. She worked as a nurse and midwife in various Nyasaland hospitals from the late 1940s up to 1966. In 1949 she met and married Joseph Mondon – my father. She had three children with Joe over a period of five years. In birth order her children are Suzanne, Richard and Katherine.

Living and working in Africa during that time was not for the faint of heart or those of weak disposition. Life was raw and full of many dangers. Medical care was rudimentary at best and tropical diseases rampant. However, Jean's twenty years of living and working in Africa were to furnish her with experience that proved invaluable for her work in the Republic of Yemen later in her life.

My father Joe Mondon was of French extraction and came from the Seychelles islands in the middle of the Indian Ocean. He and many other young Seychellois men had joined the British Army at the outbreak of World War II. After the war he worked for the British Colonial Service in Africa – this was how he came to be in Nyasaland and how he met my mother. Post-independence from Britain in 1966 our whole family left Malawi and moved to the Seychelles. Jean then worked in the main hospital on the island of Mahé for a period of time. Sadly, Joe was diagnosed with terminal bone cancer three years after arriving in Seychelles and died early in 1969. He was only forty-six years old. Jean decided to move herself and Richard and Katherine to England. Her own parents were now elderly and she wanted her two younger children to have the opportunities for further education that were available in England. The move took place just before Christmas 1969: Richard was seventeen and Katherine fourteen at the time. I was nineteen and in the process of emigrating to the USA.

Making the transition back to the UK was difficult. Not only were there huge cultural changes for the family to get used to but money was very tight. Joe had died without a will and so his estate had to be settled in Seychelles and this took years to resolve. In the meantime, Jean had to find work, get the children into school and find a place to live all at the same time. The move took place in mid-winter which, after decades of tropical living, was quite a challenge. For a few weeks, the family lacked all but the most basic items of warm clothing. With a bank loan, Jean purchased a modest two-storey home on the outskirts of Shrewsbury. She started work as a ward nurse in the hospital where she had trained during the war, but within a short time had taken the initiative to retrain as a health visitor – a role that equates to primary health care in the community.

She settled down into English life again and reconnected with her old friends. By this time I was married and living in the USA. My brother Richard was the first of my siblings to finish school and go on to university; he was followed by my sister Katherine three years later. Jean's job as a mother was done. All the chicks were out of the nest and flying on their own. Now was her chance to do what she wanted with the rest of her life.

She wasted no time. In 1974 she signed up to join the British Army and worked in Germany for two years in the role of an army health visitor. By this time, my brother Richard had returned to Africa – to work as a civil engineer in what was Rhodesia (now Zimbabwe). Encouraged by Richard's move, Jean decided take up a health visitor's post in the south of that country. This was in 1978, during the period when Rhodesia was isolated from international society because its ruling white government had declared unilateral independence from the UK. After a year in Zimbabwe she returned home to Shropshire, and settled down to a life of retirement: walking with friends; doing creative sewing and learning to paint; studying for a degree by distance-learning (through the British Open University); and traveling, both within Europe and overseas – the latter mainly to visit Richard and his family in South Africa, and myself and my husband Dennis in the USA.

However, within a few years, the itch for excitement started up again. By this time Jean was sixty-two – she decided she had one last big adventure in her and signed up as a volunteer midwife with a British group similar to the Peace Corps, and in 1984 went to what was then North

Yemen. (Together with the territory of what was then South Yemen, this is now the Republic of Yemen, or just Yemen. However, throughout the book, the term 'Yemen' on its own refers to old North Yemen. At the time of going to press, civil war rages across Yemen, and a large proportion of its population is at risk of starvation.)

This book is about Jean's adventures in Yemen told through her diaries and family letters that she wrote during that time. Chapters 2 to 5 are her observations during her early months in Yemen. Subsequent chapters are in chronological order, from mid-1984 through to her departure from Yemen two years later. Her writing presents a blow-by-blow description of her experiences, both good and bad, with no sugar coating. Jean now speaks in her own voice to tell the story of this extraordinary period in her life.

Two

Arrival in Yemen – the Sana'a Scene

Jean arrives in Sana'a in February 1984, capital of what was then North Yemen. She notes in her diary that the city 'lies in a wide valley surrounded by dun-colored mountain peaks standing out starkly like cardboard cut-outs above a blanket of brown smog hovering over the city.' The population of Sana'a in 1984 was around 425,000. Jean traveled from the UK to Yemen initially in the company of another woman volunteer, Fiona.

Dear Family,

I have taken the opportunity to send this fat letter with an Oxfam representative who is traveling back to the UK shortly. It will be mailed from there. It is not wise to use negative adjectives in normal post from here! And I wish to speak freely.

I have been here just over two weeks and it seems much longer. I hardly know where to begin or what to start with – everything seems so alien and so far from one's own ordered society.

We have been kindly received and well cared for by others in our own group – Oxfam, Peace Corps people and volunteers from CRS [Catholic Relief Services] who are just finishing earthquake relief. As an old colonial I find it ironic that we meet (on the whole) only expatriates to begin with. They have welcomed us as well as they can. We haven't met any Yemanis socially to date, except perhaps our language teacher Kokab, a charming twenty-two-year-old from the south (Aden) who speaks English and is waiting for a chance to study in the USA.

As we were driven along the road from the airport to the city, all sorts of vehicles rushed from one traffic light to another, pulling up sharply, hands on hooters as if to hurry along the green light. When it did appear they all rushed forward like race horses from their starting pens. Their impatience was so great that I was vaguely surprised to see them actually obeying the traffic lights. We noticed many unfinished buildings and piles of rubble and I wondered when we would arrive at the real, finished city, but we never did. The whole place gives off an air of chaos and ruin that resembles the aftermath of an air raid with nobody interested in repair work.

The main streets that we have seen are paved. The most noticeable thing about them is the large public rubbish bins situated every 200 yards or so, to which people carry their trash, and herds of sheep and goats scavenge amongst the overflow. It appears that rubbish collection is a fairly recent innovation and occurs about once a week, leaving a trail of malodorous excess garbage on the site of each bin. Off these main streets are unpaved narrow, litter-strewn alleyways leading to residential areas and our own two houses. As we pick our way from one house to the other we catch glimpses of several charming courtyards through cracks in the formidable metal doors guarding each one. It seems to be a place of public squalor and private affluence.

We see small camel trains carrying firewood, and always a sad little donkey tied to the last camel's tail. The city is full of traffic and hooting and the sound of the call to prayer. It is high up, at around 7,000 feet. There have been no good rains for several years, so it is incredibly dry and dusty. We are not short of water in our house but we are very careful with it. We see very little in the way of imported goods of the type and quality we take for granted; most stuff is Indian, Chinese and Japanese.

The house we are now occupying is quite old and had belonged to a Jewish merchant. A heavy wooden door with archaic catches, latches and locks opens onto the alley. If someone bangs on this door you can look down from the flat roof, and, if it is a friend, you pull a rope that disengages one of the bolts – forerunner of today's intercom. Once inside, you step down into a dark room used as a store out of which steep, uneven stone steps lead upward, and at each bend an unventilated cupboard is let into the thick wall. I believe such spaces were used as bedrooms but now are store cupboards. Upstairs are two bedrooms, a primitive bathroom and kitchen – whose concrete sink slopes away from the plug hole – a temperamental electricity and water supply, and a rough roof-top space where we hang our clothes to dry and enjoy the view onto other roof gardens, courtyards used by families and animals, and the nearby passages and streets.

Most houses have a garden courtyard surrounded by a block wall, their entrances often having large double doors made of heavy metal and painted in colorful designs. These doors seem to be a specialty of Yemen; one sees door-makers in all villages and outskirts, and the doors are displayed on the roadside. The locks are also special. You need inside knowledge in order to be able to use them. Something else they specialize in are very attractive designs of colored glass which are fitted above windows and doors. However, the pretty doors are often twisted and warped and can be very difficult and noisy to open and shut.

Each morning at four we are awakened by the 'dawn chorus' of muezzins calling from every mosque; when one stops another starts, as if they are talking to each other. Most mornings are bright and the sun shines through the arched windows, showing off their insets of colored glass.

We were keen to explore the city before the rigors of the language school set in. So, having armed ourselves with a city map, we walked to the post office for stamps and postcards. We drank black, cinnamon-flavored tea in a small cafe. The noisy traffic-laden streets are dusty and have broken, uneven pavements and no drainage, but it is dry at the moment. All sorts of filth such as paper, plastic bags, tins, heaps of used khat leaves, old shoes and rags are lying about, and, of course, the goats wander around scavenging. [Khat is the leaf of a shrub grown extensively in the Arabian Peninsula, where it is widely chewed as a stimulant. Jean makes frequent references to it during her letters.] The shops had opened their large, painted metal doors to reveal dimly lit caverns of brightly colored merchandise. Returning home we were obliged to weave our way through lines of wet washing hung across the pavement. Tony [the group's project coordinator] tells us it is the local laundry and inquired if we had seen his red shirt there!

Back at our house, as we tried to do our washing, we soon discovered the plumbing deficiencies. It seems that most houses have water tanks on the roof that have to be filled by a hand pump down below, and there are problems with airlocks if you allow it to run dry. We are learning.

That first evening Tony invited eight people round to meet us: Americans, Dutch, Burmese and Brits, all working on aid projects mainly to do with water supplies for the areas recently devastated by earthquakes. The following day we were invited to a lunch party by Tony who lives in a most attractive new house, built Yemeni style with large rooms and windows, and in a walled garden with thick walls. The colorful furnishings and decorative artifacts were all of local origin. The vegetarian food at lunch was delicious. From there we were escorted to the British Embassy to meet a consular official and on by bus to the old city and the souk.

The old houses of Sana'a and the souk

I had read about the old houses of Sana'a but to be here and see them piled up behind the huge crumbling city walls is an amazing experience. The bus put us down at Bab Al Yemen – the imposing entrance to the souk and the old city. On either side of this busy thoroughfare were food vendors cooking on Primus stoves. Delicious smells tempted us to try the crisply fried slivers of liver and the kebabs. Other entrepreneurs had set up juice extractors on tables and processed fresh lime juice to order. Inside the gates we found a labyrinth of narrow, dark, dirt passages thronged with hooting motor bikes, small lorries and cars, as well as donkey and camel transport. Crowds of people, mainly Arabs in various costumes, were gesticulating, arguing, fighting, spitting, and all were in a hurry. These alleys are flanked by small brightly lit caverns of merchandise, especially fabrics. I have never seen so many sumptuous materials in one small place – embroidered velvets, spangled voiles, brilliant silks and taffetas. Several shops stocked glamorous kaftans from all over the Arab world and India; I bought two cotton ones for three pounds each which I hope will be useful in the village.

Towering above these small shops are the famous, fabulous houses of old Sana'a. They are constructed of sun-baked mud bricks, seven to eight storeys high, each storey having its own unique design in white stucco around the windows of colored glass, the balustraded balconies and over-hanging window shades. All together these features give the appearance of a huge iced cake or a piece of richly embroidered cloth. Because of the seething mass around me I was unable to spend much time gazing at this scene. When I did lift my head I was assailed by a flash of huge excitement at being able to view the splendid yet barbaric scene of this ancient city unconcerned with imposed principles of symmetry, just standing there in all its higgeldy-piggeldy grandeur. It brought to my mind Flecker's poem *The Golden Road To Samarkand*, which has haunted and beckoned me since my youth.

Further on were, in separate areas, open bags of colored spices with their distinctive pungent odors and gunny sacks of a variety of pulses and grains. Then the vegetable and meat stalls, the hubble-bubble parlors and everywhere crowds of animated Eastern characters in their traditional dress. We saw no other foreigners. Off these alleyways, narrow dark passages curved away to mysterious corners in which, I imagine, one could easily get lost. I have learned the phrase 'where is Bab Al Yemen please' in Arabic as a precaution.

Eventually we arrived at Tony's old house – a real gem – with heavy, carved wooden doors, narrow, deep, uneven stone stairs up the center of the house leading to the living quarters on the fifth floor. This stairway, like the one in our house, has these intriguing cupboards or niches let into the wall where the steps make a turn. Tony himself is an architect with fine artistic sense. In his kitchen he is repairing exquisite lattice-work window shutters made by the Jews 200 years ago. The reception room or *muffrage* has no extraneous bits of furniture to detract from its simple arrangements of thick white walls and archways, apart from a few rugs on the floor surrounded by large, colorful cushions. Above the wide unglazed windows are fan-shaped colored-glass insets over which a delicate, curving line had been molded. From here we looked out on and into the fairy-tale houses already described and up to the craggy, bare brown mountains beyond.

Toilet arrangements in Yemen

But now I must move on to more mundane and basic matters – for however splendid or exotic a house may be, lavatories are essential and sometimes guests need to use them. On request I was shown a small, dark room and instructed in the use of the two holes: one for urine, the other for solids. As the holes were several feet apart I was relieved that I only needed to urinate. I could not imagine my aim being sufficiently accurate for the other hole. One must not use paper for personal cleaning. There is always a supply of clean water in a small jug. It appears that the solids go down a long black hole (we were several storeys high) to a reservoir of solids from other sources which dry and consolidate over the years; they are eventually removed and used as fuel in the public baths. I was amazed to find there was very little smell from this archaic system.

An unusual restaurant

On our way home we came upon a rough sign by a hole in the wall on which the word 'Restaurant' had been laboriously written. It looked unconventional enough to warrant a visit and I was not disappointed. We stepped down into a dark cave-like room furnished with a few low, rickety tables surrounded by male customers. I then became aware of the kitchen area where huge pots bubbled away on Primus stoves. It all looked quite filthy. I could hardly believe the scene was real or that I was there and prepared to eat.

We were greeted like honored guests, being salaamed while at the same time there was a hurried discussion about where we should sit. Then, quick as lightening, some narrow, rickety steps were let down which one of the waiters shinned up to open shutters and effect a quick whip around with a dirty, multi-purpose cloth he kept around his neck. As we were conducted to the 'upper room' the biblical story of the Last Supper came to mind. In this upper room were several long, low trestle tables with even lower benches on which one was supposed to sit cross-legged during the meal time. By this time I had decided to give up my inhibitions and enjoy the experience. If I was to survive in Yemen I must be prepared to do so. We were served bubbling fenugreek paste and flat, hot bread to dip into it, but I didn't care for this slimy, green, tasteless stuff. As we left the restaurant we looked up to see the old houses of the city in a ghostly pile enlivened by the many lit-up colored windows. It was a day to remember.

Travel papers and visas

Now that our initial-arrival excitement has simmered down we have been experiencing some of the frustrations of living and working here. Getting entry visas in London is one thing, but, having arrived, many other formalities have to be gone through that involve visits to various perplexing government offices. They are perplexing to us because there appears to be no form of hierarchy, no way of distinguishing which offices house august officials. Off the wide, dusty passages, in which loiter an assortment of unidentifiable characters, scruffy, battered doors open into equally squalid, unimpressive offices. Whenever we found our essential official he would be in a hurry. Our conversations with him were continually interrupted by obsequious favor-seekers carrying scraps of paper to be signed.

We have started language lessons for two hours a day; we also read reports on our own and learn about other foreign aid projects, studying the map for their locations. Then, last week, the big moment arrived when we were to visit our designated posts. Mine is in a desert village, Abs, fifty miles from the Red Sea and just south of the Saudi border, and Fiona's is in a remote area, where her group will live in an old Turkish fort on a mountain top.

Love, Mum

Three

OUR FIRST YEMENI ROAD TRIP – VISIT
TO ABS AND AL HODEIDAH

Dear Family,

Having obtained our travel passes, copies of passports and letters explaining who we are, to be given to the many military observation posts along the road, we were taken early one morning to the bus depot outside the old city walls of Sana'a. Here we found the bus entrance blocked by a gesticulating, elbowing, noisy crowd, all anxious for the best seats. We, of course, hung back and were rewarded by being courteously conducted to the front seat.

The long-distance buses are well-maintained French vehicles with tinted windows. The journey to Al Hodeidah on the Red Sea coast took about six hours during which there was one 'comfort' stop at a rough wayside cafe. As the bus drew up we noticed the waiter hurriedly flicking the tables with his multi-purpose shoulder-cloth. Here we had black tea and dry bread. We were desperate for a loo [bathroom] and were obliged to go to the village outskirts and squat behind one of the many ruined buildings. In front of us, some fifty yards away, the male passengers were doing the same while staring onto the wide, deep valley at their feet. They knew what we were doing but ignored us completely, while we, on the other hand, were reassured by their presence. The bus would not go on without them.

Among the other passengers were a few Yemeni ladies vomiting quietly under their black veils into plastic bags which were then thrown out of the window. Many men wore colorful headdresses and wide, finely beaded and embroidered belts with a curved jambia [a short dagger, the handle of which indicates the status of the wearer] stuck in front, as well as a small machine gun across the chest.

The splendid road we traveled on, built and maintained by the Chinese, snakes its way through massive, craggy mountains and deep valleys. The scenery we passed reminded me of pictures I have seen of the North West Frontier in India and the Khyber Pass. Two or three times during the trip soldiers boarded the bus and demanded to see our passports. We were quite terrified, never expecting to get them back, but... no problem.

Along the way, we saw old villages whose mud-brick houses blend so perfectly with the surrounding countryside that they are almost invisible until you are amongst them. Lower down, fertile terraced valleys growing maize, fruit and vegetables gradually merge with the plastic-bag littered desert that surrounds the unattractive port of Al Hodeidah.

The bus stopped twice during the trip to collect alms from the passengers for disabled people on the roadside. Every twenty miles or so there were metal tanks of water for travelers. However, today Evian water has come to the rescue in Yemen, with a beautiful, modern water-bottling plant. As far as I'm concerned it's the best thing I could imagine. Probably not the correct way of ensuring pure water for all. But someone got onto a good thing there. Yemenis love it and so do I. One can drink water without fear. On one of the stops on that hot journey the conductor gave all the ladies a drink. We chose a small, cold 'Shamlan' – trade name of this water. Unfortunately Yemen is littered with empty, squashed, non-biodegradable Shamlan bottles.

At Al Hodeidah we joined another bus of friendly passengers for a two-hour journey to Abs during which time more bottles of water were passed around, and most people enjoyed chewing khat leaves which were plucked from small branches bought off traders along the road. The driver and his mate were extremely cooperative about the khat trading stops and showed great interest and expertise in the quality of the leaves. We were not at all sure where to get off. The countryside all along appeared to be equally scruffy and devoid of landmarks. It lacked the pure outlines of real desert, being peppered with dusty, dry, shriveled shrubs and bushes decorated with rubbish. We need not have worried, as the driver knew who we were and where we were going, and of course, we were met by team members in Abs.

The village of Abs

The village of Abs is more or less what I expected but imagination can never replace reality, and we were overwhelmed with the ugliness and wretchedness of the area. It's like a big transport stop on the main road to Saudi Arabia. Abs is in a perpetual dust storm with plastic and paper bags covering the ground for a mile around. It was hot and dusty and by then I was extremely hungry plus had a headache. I felt beaten up and defeated after the long journey, new situations, my shortage of language skills, and never quite knowing how to behave – I was anxious not to offend. Sometime later, after I had assuaged my worst hunger-pangs with dry bread, it was announced that we were all ready to go to Shaffa'a to eat. Shaffa'a, unlike Abs which is half a mile from the main road, is right on this busy highway and halfway between Al Hodeidah and the Saudi Arabian border. This location has led to a proliferation of restaurants, vehicle repair shops, petrol stations and shops full of brightly colored junky merchandise. This place fascinates me. I had imagined Abs to be a lonely outpost, far away from the center of world events. But this adjacent strip of ugly entrepreneurial development was full of movement, color, clamor of blacksmiths' hammers, revving engines of huge, brightly painted lorries laden with mysterious goods, and buses pulling in and disgorging hungry travelers who scattered to various restaurants and shops shouting to each other. All this vibrant activity caused me to review my preconceptions. I suppose the center of the world for individuals is always where one happens to be. Not to feel thus must indicate a measure of alienation or homesickness.

Our group have their favorite eating spot, set back off the roadside to give random parking space. The eating area had around thirty tables and chairs; behind it was the kitchen, where Primus stoves and open fires roared away under huge steaming pots and bread ovens. The kitchen staff, in their ragged clothes held together by broad dagger-holding belts, danced prompt and civil attendance on us. Between the eating area and the car park a semicircular laager had been created by bedsteads on which men were reclining chewing khat, smoking hookah pipes and discoursing with friends. Amongst all this, itinerant merchants hawked their goods and a shouting, gesticulating mad woman, to whom no one paid attention, wove her erratic way. In spite of its ugliness, Shaffa'a pleased me; perhaps it was only the food, but I felt all was not lost if I could come here occasionally and be part of the big, bad world again. Even so, as I lay on my bed under the stars that night, I just could not believe it all or imagine how I could live here and for a short while, desperation overcame me.

After a night's sleep my natural optimism returned with the sunrise. Our compound has recently been created by a local businessman cashing in on the influx of foreign workers. It follows the traditional idea of the extended family living area, where many beehive-shaped huts are enclosed behind tall mud walls. But in our case, the houses and walls are constructed of concrete blocks, although we do have the obligatory brightly colored metal gate entrance. The compound is well kept; heavy sand has been laid down, trees have been planted, and rubbish disposal is treated with great fastidiousness (rightly so). Squat-type, outdoor latrines and the bathing area (a shower) occupy a small bricked-off corner. Toilet paper has to be burned in a container. Our cloths are soaked in a bucket with soap powder, and the water is then used to wash down the toilets.

The kitchen is adequate, having a bottled propane gas-fired fridge and stove, a good table and sink. However, we wash dishes in a bowl so that the used water can be fed to a few newly planted trees. The bedrooms are so hot that we all sleep outside under mosquito nets hung from the clothes line. I am told the water is of good quality, coming from deep wells nearby. It is delivered to us by a small tanker, the owner of which lives next door. He pumps the water into a large tank in the yard and we must then pump it up into another tank on the roof – so there is plenty of scope for contamination. Electricity is supplied, spasmodically, from 6:00 p.m. to 10:00 p.m.

We spent several days in Abs during which time my companion Fiona became very ill with a severe chest infection – she was in bed for three days and very depressed. I felt a bit desperate the first evening. I hoped I would be able to cope although part of me thought I could never ever live there. I took comfort in thinking, 'if it gets me down I'll not stay.'

During this stay, I went out with the others to visit the local government clinic, which is about one hundred yards along a wide, dusty track – it is the base of our activities and is a dreary collection of block rooms in a sandy yard. A broken ambulance lies on its side in one corner; there is a muddy patch in another from where a water tap gives, sporadically, the only water for the compound. In spite of this, I was astonished to witness Ayesha, the cleaning lady, using an electric washing machine. She carried water by bucket from the tap to the machine.

Dressed in flowing, wispy black robes, and having hennaed, long-nailed hands and feet, this lady resembles a Welsh witch. Her hair, also hennaed a bright orange, is bound up with a black voile scarf on top of which sits a tall conical straw hat. She marches around the yard making sure nothing exciting escapes her attention or advice, always adjusting the long scarf she wears round her neck.

Apart from Ayesha's running commentary, greetings and orders, I was surprised to find the clinic so quiet. I expected the throngs I had seen in Africa and Seychelles, but this sad and mournful place does not seem popular. The doctor is a Sudanese supported by several Somali and

Sudanese medical assistants, and there are two wards of six beds each for short-stay cases. No surgery can be done here apart from minor suturing and dressings. Our main function in the clinic is to create a room where women can come and be seen by a woman. Up until now they have come with a male member of the family who makes sure the male doctor does not touch her or have any of her clothes removed. Her 'moral purity' is far more important than her physical health it seems.

The main object of the project is to try to improve family health with special reference to that of women and children. The midwife's role is to become acquainted with the traditional birth attendants in a quiet way, to gain their confidence so that they will help disperse the good news of immunization, antenatal care and family planning. Abs was chosen for this project because of the low standard of health in the local population who are amongst the poorest in Yemen. At the same time, a new clinic is being built but frequently the money sources dry up and the building ceases.

Later I was taken visiting to the poorest part of the village, a collection of flimsy huts and tarpaulin lean-tos. My guide talked and joked with the women while giving the health messages and I was awestruck by her command of Arabic. We went on to visit an American Peace Corps water scheme a few miles out in the desert. Their foreman lives and sleeps on his bags of cement on which we were invited to sit and enjoy Cokes opened by the butt of his Kalashnikov rifle. We finished the day with a scenic tour of the desolate countryside. We returned via the souk where I bought rice and onions and concocted a pilaf which brought me some temporary popularity.

Our compound is on the edge of the village which is expanding rapidly. One reason for this expansion is that Abs acts as a conduit for the khat leaves that are brought down daily from the adjacent mountains. I am told that some of the best khat grows up there at a wild, remote place with the splendid name of Marharbisha. I look forward to visiting that place so that I can say, in an off-hand manner, 'the other day when I was in Marharbisha....'

Abs itself occupies quite a small compact area, probably a quarter-mile square, which is criss-crossed by many narrow, winding, sandy passages. On either side are the tall mud walls enclosing the family compounds. I could easily get lost in these alleyways which eventually end at the village outskirts from where dusty tracks lead off, either into the dark, forbidding no-man's land or to the rubbish dumps on which live packs of scavenging savage dogs and several sick or injured donkeys. The daily, permanent souk is a collection of makeshift tables and holes in walls occupying a few passages and covered by old tarpaulins or rough thatch. From these rickety stalls one can buy essentials such as potatoes, onions, rice, small bruised bananas and blocks of glistening, sticky dates – these covered in flies. The weekly, itinerant souk occupies the main track into the village and offers a wider variety of vegetables and spices, and a large selection of brightly colored metal plates and trays that are used as decorations inside the circular mud houses. I saw lots of gaudy clothing, painted boxes and trunks for the migrant workers, and all sorts of trinkets and sweetmeats. Amongst these piles of merchandise small, noisy motor bikes toured around touting for pillion passengers for the main road or to Shaffa'a. I noticed several carrying a sheep between the passenger and the driver.

Two days after our arrival in Abs, it had been arranged that we should go on to the mountain project but on the way there, at Al Hodeidah, news reached us that our house in Sana'a had been broken into and our bags ransacked. We were obliged to return to Sana'a immediately. I was fairly philosophical about this news; in a way I was almost relieved to have an excuse to leave the dreariness I had witnessed on all sides. At that moment I didn't feel I could face the uncertainties of a visit to the group who operate from an old Turkish fort on the mountain top.

When we arrived back in Sana'a we found our bedrooms ransacked and desolate and several people running around fixing locks. I had lost many small items, and my beautiful new Lark suitcase – which I had bought with Suzanne in Los Gatos [California] – had been ripped open even though not locked. I was relieved to find my Gore-Tex jacket and hiking boots intact. As a consolation we were taken out to dinner at a restaurant whose tables wore well-laundered white cloths and were lit by candles. The food was not as good as at the wayside cafes. For the next two days I was ill with a chest cold and upset tummy and Sana'a was enveloped in clouds of filthy dust.

If you could see me here you wouldn't believe it – but I'm still the same inside. It's amazing what you can get used to. So far it's been a succession of readjustments to a lower standard of living materially, although one can shower twice a day and keep hair clean. I smile when I look at the hair dryer, curling tongues, silver hair color and the fine-water face spray. What a joke – if you used the spray here your face would drip mud! I'm still using my special shampoo and face soap. Don't know how long that will last.

I hope you all enjoy this letter – written when I should have been doing Arabic study.

Love, Mum

Four

SANA'A – CULTURAL ORIENTATION AND VISITS
TO OTHER FOREIGN AID PROJECTS

Dear Family,

We have started language lessons with a young woman from Aden and continue going around government offices with Lenore, a fluent Arabist, who is endeavoring to get insurance and a license for a car. This is a tricky business in a place where most people drive without either. Out in the country, children who can barely reach the steering wheel are seen driving powerful vehicles. I was impressed by the beautiful girls working in these offices and wearing modern Arab dress of a long white trench coat, black silk blouse and long skirt. We looked cheap and scruffy beside them. On my way back, on foot, I met two camels and a donkey tied nose to tail, loaded with firewood, being led by a white-bearded character right out of the Old Testament.

Because the 'official' language school has not yet started I will be making visits to other foreign projects while Fiona will attempt to get up to her mountain-top destination. Preparations for my next foray into the unknown are progressing slowly, depending on a functioning telephone and responses from my hosts, who are to be the Norwegians at Ibb. At the same time Mandy and her American friends organized an outing to the hill-top villages of Thula and Kokaban. Thula, once a strategic, fortified outpost, since destroyed by earthquakes, is now deserted. Goats with their herd boys roam among the graves and tumbledown buildings; here and there, at useful points, stand lookout towers in ruins. We climbed to the top of the biggest tower. From here we looked down onto a huge rocky surface into which deep caverns had been excavated by hand for use as food storage. The entrance holes appeared to be very small compared to the excavated area underneath, big enough for a man to pass through. One wonders how many died in there or went mad with claustrophobia while excavating. There must have been covers for those holes when storage was their function. From another angle, the high cliff wall fell away almost vertically, giving us splendid views over vast dun-colored, terraced plains and bright-green patches of gardens near an inhabited village below, where people were sitting on the flat roofs.

On top here at Thula, among the graves, wild flowers, birds and silence, I was reminded of Spion Kop in South Africa, where other graves lie on a wild, deserted, remote mountain top, left entirely to the hand of nature. Kokaban, whose stark surroundings reminded me of the Grand Canyon, is sparsely inhabited and must have known better days because of the impressive ruins of Parthenon-like city gates and the remains of a huge stone water cistern with steps and ledges cut into its sides; there must have been more rain in former times.

We were given a lift in the back of a pick-up truck. The young man, having asked Mandy our ages, said he would take her and throw the two old ones away!

In our spare time Fiona and I try to keep the house clean and cook some good food. We even tried the sticky dates first seen in Abs and swore never to eat. They are good. We enjoyed the food and company of a lively French group at our house one evening; we also visited the embassy club for lunch by the pool, and the museum, where several parents were explaining the historical exhibits to their children. Yemenis we have met appear to be proud and pleased with their recent move away from the despotic rule of imams.

We made another excursion to the souk where I bought an old alabaster candle holder. Early one morning six of us went to the Sheraton for breakfast – as much as you like for thirty-three rials – where they had every breakfast food apart from pork products.

The other day I had a really super time. I took one of the many small buses to the post office. I managed to exchange a few words in Arabic with the other passengers, and made myself understood at the post office. I went into one of the many pharmacies where I observed people receiving intravenous injections across the counter. On my way back to Al Ghar I espied a tray of bean stew, steaming, in small pots being carried to some offices. It smelled delicious and looked so attractive with its sprinkling of green onions on top that I followed the bearer back to his base, a small street cafe, where I had a gastronomic treat. I was delighted with my adventure and I am, at least momentarily, enjoying being a vagabond and no longer notice the rubbish.

Another charming experience was a bird-watching trip to Hadda, about eight miles from Sana'a, where we walked through a wadi of apricot trees, heard the tuneful song of Yemeni linnets, watched sunbirds darting in and out of foliage, and hoopoes and babblers jumping about under trees. I was suddenly overtaken by a wave of homesickness and surprise as I heard willow warblers, in a thick fig tree, singing their sweet, familiar descending song just as they do in Europe.

Later that day I was taken to tea at the Al Hamd Palace Hotel by a member of our group who wanted to give me more information about the Abs Project – and what might be expected of me there – without the inevitable interruptions at the house. The hotel used to be one of the imams' palaces. We were taken onto the roof for the view over the surrounding gardens, and then to the *muffrage* with its brilliant cushions and wall hangings. On the way back we bought a mop for the house – back to basics!

The following day we had to rush around labyrinthine offices to get our visas extended, collect travel passes and do lots of photocopying;

later, we dined well at a Lebanese restaurant on kebabs, bulgur wheat, tomato and parsley salad, hummus and rice pudding.

As you can tell, we have widely differing experiences here ranging from the sublime to the obnoxious or worse, and today was no exception. I was pleased to be leaving the squalid transit house for a few days and its gruesome approach road upon which a dead cat had been lying for days affording hilarious target practice for stone-throwing children.

Khat-chew party

Before going to Ibb I attended a khat chew at an American Embassy home just outside the city. A 'chew' is the Yemeni equivalent to our cocktail party but at an earlier hour, usually from 4:00 p.m. to 7:00 p.m. The house, set in dusty scrub, had an unimpressive appearance from outside, being dark and squat, but on entering I was transported to a fairy-tale world. The *muffrage*, where we sat on cushions of silver, gold and richly colored brocade and velvets, had a rug in the center upon which a huge brocaded serpent lay coiled up. There were, of course, bundles of khat for the chew, brass spittoons, elegant hookah pipes, incense burners and many low, well-shaded brass lamps. We sat around on the cushions and were supposed to chew those leaves! But it didn't appeal to me. The chap beside me kept giving me choice leaves, tender young ones, which I just kept in my mouth and spat out later. Nearly all Yemeni men chew khat in the afternoons; they have a ball of it inside the cheek. They look as if they all have abscesses or deformities. The ball of leaves is as big as an egg. I went to this party with my Arabic teacher and her American boyfriend who have been so kind to me. In other rooms I noticed wooden chests inlaid with mother-of-pearl, and lighted alcoves in which hung pieces of Yemeni jewelry. There were, of course, the usual tall windows topped by crescents of colored glass. Other guests included several Yemeni university students who harangued us on the evils of western society. I had the impression they were not happy with the presence of foreign aid workers in their country, especially those who could not speak Arabic. I kept quiet, having a sneaking sympathy with their point of view.

Later, on the wide moonlit verandah, as we bade farewell to our host – who had been suitably dressed in Arab style – I looked back into those magical rooms, while outside a full moon sailed up behind the jagged black mountain that was sharply etched against the shining, deep-indigo sky. I shall never forget that enchanted evening.

Trip to Ibb

The next morning I set off on my journey to Ibb, which is about four hours drive south of Sana'a and half way to Taiz which is near the border with South Yemen. After waiting for the initial chaos of bus-loading, I was given a front seat beside an elderly white-robed, turbaned gentleman with a horrible loose cough which he made no effort to conceal. In fact, he seemed quite proud of it. After each good productive cough, he expectorated into the corner of a beautiful Cashmere shawl which was draped across his shoulders and then, delicately, he tied it up as if it were a precious gift. Having ascertained I was a medical person, he produced X-rays, a barium-meal report and diagnosis of 'shadows on the lung' in English. At one bus stop, on seeing a friend out in the street, he jumped up excitedly while at the same time depositing his charming bundle on my lap. On the return journey I sat by another chesty chap but I didn't look to see what he did with the product of his condition, but he did invoke Allah with every coughing bout!

The clinic here, run by the Norwegian Save the Children organization, is finely situated on top of a conical hill. Yesterday I saw the director and chief medical officer looking down on the square below – about half a mile away. I joined them. The square was packed with people. It was a public execution! The victim stood in the back of an open truck. Two shots rang out. He fell; the truck took off at speed. I couldn't believe it. I don't think you should advertise these things to too many people. It seemed bizarre, to say the least, that such a scene can pass before your eyes and then one carries on with life's normal humdrum activities.

The two Scandinavian nurses I stayed with run an efficient and popular family-planning clinic combined with ante- and postnatal work and home visiting. They live in a large, comfortable house just outside the town, are keen cooks, and have a neat garden of vegetables, zinnias, hollyhocks, roses and marigolds. I have enjoyed cooking for them and myself in their nice kitchen. One of the girls has a Lebanese boyfriend who was picked up by the police for having no passport at a checkpoint last weekend. No one knows where he is. She is distracted and helpless. Stupid to travel without documents in such a country. There are checkpoints every fifty miles or so. You never know when they may want to see the passport. I've had to show mine every time.

From the house one looks onto a flat area of cultivated gardens waiting for rain, neatly divided by sandy paths and dusty trees. Beyond is the town, about half a mile away, which rises up to the conical hill; outlined on top of the hill are the pillars of a ruined building, slightly reminiscent of parts of Athens. Beyond again is a bare brown rocky mountain on which one can see houses perched at intervals all the way to the top, which at night looks as if it is laced with fairy lights.

Later on I was taken to the nearby ancient, tumbledown city of Jibla that has the dusty remains of a palace once lived in by a Queen Arwa. Nearby we visited a well-established, busy American Baptist hospital. This was a scene I recognized from my active nursing life in Africa and I had a longing to cast off my dowdy dress, put on a nurse's uniform and get stuck into some real work! I was invited to join them if I couldn't settle in Abs. I spent a pleasant week in Ibb observing this well-run clinic that we hope to emulate in Abs, with special reference to their methods of crowd control, and dissemination of health messages in the children's clinic. In our off-duty time there, we visited other members of the international community. We also went to a Yemeni women's party where we were served Coke, orangeade, sweets, chewing gum, popcorn, fig rolls and sweet tea. We were obliged to join in the dancing amidst incessant giggling, leaving at 6:00 p.m. I was enjoying myself enormously when a peremptory call came from our office in Sana'a asking when did I propose returning? So the next morning I was once more delivered onto the bus and went back to Sana'a.

So far I remain well, no pain in the hip or headaches, except when I travel long distances without food.

Many thanks to you both for letters. All the best to you Suzanne in your new venture. I am sure you will succeed. Pleased to hear you are enjoying your work and company Katherine.

I am scribbling this before I leave Abs for Diane, an American woman, to take to Cyprus.

Write soon.

Love, Mum

Five

Country Tour

The country tour was the next item on our protracted orientation exercise. I was to go with two younger women, one of whom has been in the country two years, so knows something about it and the language. Even so, throughout the tour they both showed a marked reluctance to get on the road each morning. At last, one day at 11:00 a.m. we set off for Rada, where we were to visit another Scandinavian project. Our journey took us south on the busy main road towards Taiz through the now-familiar, stark mountainous terrain as far as Dhamar where we turned east towards the sparsely inhabited South Yemen border. Along this quieter road I noticed a marked change in the landscape towards a pure, clean desert of wide valleys, smoothly sculptured low hills and clear sparkling air, while far beyond lay serried ridges of blue, mauve and pink mountains. The houses also were of a lighter color; some had whimsical spikes on top. I felt a distinct lifting of my spirits.

Our hosts lived comfortably in well-appointed first-floor flats from where one looked out across irrigated fields towards the walls of the village in the center of which an old crumbling Turkish fort sat on a rocky prominence. Later on, as the sun was setting, I looked across those fields and saw a long camel train slowly winding its way from the vast, uncluttered desert through a small hole in the wall and into the village, where one imagined them bivouacking beside their bulky mysterious loads.

The following day, I accompanied a nurse on a visit to new mothers who are encouraged to breastfeed, and eventually attend the clinic for immunizations and family-planning advice. Most interesting for me was visiting three-day-old babies, checking them all over and seeing how they were feeding. Women here stay home for forty days after delivery. As with our own role in Abs, one of the most important aspects of the work of these expatriate nurses is to find local women to act as counterparts who would accompany them, helping to translate health messages and eventually taking over from them. It is not easy to find women willing and able to do this in such a small, conservative and patriarchal society. The counterparts have to be from among those who have nothing to lose, such as 'bride price.' They are usually divorced, widowed or elderly unmarried. We took our hosts out for a lunch of good grilled fish in the best restaurant, a rough and ready place, the floor strewn with sawdust and straw.

My traveling companions again showed reluctance to get on the road for our cross-country journey – for which we had been given the sketchiest instructions – that took us over a rough mountain road with steep, torturous passes on which the car stalled several times. We traveled three hours on this road, passing through incredibly dramatic scenery. One never ceases to be amazed at the way in which passable roads have been fashioned over the jagged mountain tops only to twist and turn endlessly and steeply to the valley floor. We came across several camel trains carrying firewood which is a precious commodity here. It is like traveling through the pages of the *National Geographic* magazine.

We arrived at our destination after dark and were escorted by a local person down a slippery, rocky bank through a broken wire fence, over household debris, filthy puddles and mangy cats to the doorway of a low, mean house. We banged on the door and after announcing who we were there was a great struggle from within to unbar bolts and undo locks.

On entering I did wonder why they bothered – who would want to get in here? Inside we found two incredibly depressed young Germans who, after three years as paramedics in the local clinic, were totally negative about everything. I felt sorry for them and was ashamed at our rudeness in arriving so late.

After a half hour of polite conversation and lengthy silences, I asked if there was a hotel we could stay in, knowing full well that there was not, but it was a way of getting round to our immediate needs. My traveling companions were of the type who will sit about for hours rather than make a decision. There was no hotel, end of story. After ten minutes I said, 'Well, we cannot go on to Ibb on that road at night,' and asked them what did they think? We were then offered a space on the floor, which was fine by us. We had our sleeping bags. However, they had no food in the house, so we all trooped off through the aforementioned rubbish to a restaurant which opened onto the main street, this being not more than a muddy track up and down which thundered laden vans and lorries. The floor of the large eating area was strewn with sawdust and at the back was a vast, dark kitchen fitfully illuminated by fires and stoves. The whole scene, together with the skinny, sweating, ragged waiters, reminded me of the Romantic artists' impressions of Ironbridge at the height of the Industrial Revolution. We were served with a large selection of unspeakable food. I nibbled at a few things that I thought would be safe. We were the only women there. Other clients were mainly tribesmen armed with machine guns or rifles. They took no notice of us.

Several times since my arrival in Yemen I have been beguiled by the promise of 'a really good restaurant.' I should know better by now. They all turn out to be crude eating places full of heat and noise with the usual lively characters dashing about with a filthy cloth over their shoulders. They slap the food down in front of you. The hot flat bread is slung on the bare table by hand. There is no pretense, all is on view. They don't need to hide unhygienic habits, because they are unaware of such inhibitions and there are no health inspectors to hide from. If I talk about food here a lot it must be because of the total lack of any other sensuous pleasures! Back at the shack I slept, unwashed, in my dear sleeping bag. I clung to it as a child does to a familiar toy or cloth.

Early the next morning I managed to break out of the fortress after weaving my way through washing hanging up to dry in this black cavern. Outside the sun was shining and the countryside appeared magical – it consisted of a series of deep, green gorges, sparkling streams, banana groves, paw paw trees and colorful birds, while on a zigzag path strings of donkeys laden with water cans walked up and down. But our hosts assured us that the beautiful valley was snake-infested and many people died from their bites.

Fortunately I had cereal with me so was able to have breakfast. The others had dry bread and jam from a dirty pot. I also had tea bags and my own cup, sheet and pillow! I have brought very few clothes with me, concentrating on more important things for my safety and well-being. Of course, I share with the others, who scorn such ideas but are happy to cash in on what I have. I always carry drinking water – they don't. Fiona is very careless and sloppy with food. She has had stomach problems for two weeks. The other girl likes chocolate, Coke, white bread and canned beans. She is full of left-wing ideas and the horrors of life in the UK. But she is also very clever in a quiet way; reads a lot and remembers what she reads. She is hoping to study when she gets back. She and Fiona are forever talking of the injustice of life in the UK. Perhaps they do it on purpose. I don't often comment but sometimes one is obliged to say something. After all, the system isn't totally evil. I keep asking them: where is their perfect society? Why don't they create it? But of course they are prevented by the Wicked Capitalists. I know there is something in what they say, but they are typical of a lot of people today who feel they are powerless to change their own lives. Coming to Yemen doesn't help because you bring yourself and your problems with you!

As I write, there is a bright-blue lizard with an orange tail on the white brick wall of the garden. I have seen beautiful blue and green bee-eater birds recently. When they fly their wings are a translucent gold; I have also seen cinnamon-breasted buntings. On the road yesterday I saw lots of little dun-colored birds with a sharp tuft on their heads. They run about like wagtails. I haven't got my bird book with me but many birds seen here are not in the East Africa book. One I have seen with a cocked tail is an Arabian babbler, I am told.

Back indoors I learned that my companions were unwell, and I am sorry to say that my first thought was of the horror if we could not get away from here! Fortunately they agreed with me that there was no point in prolonging the visit which could only act as a cautionary tale in how NOT to do things. We boarded our car with alacrity, for once, and continued to Ibb: a totally different scene there, with people working purposefully and cheerfully in a well-established project. At Ibb, apart from the obligatory visits to the clinic and lecture on its history, we enjoyed the civilized comforts of home.

One evening, I walked out into the surrounding gardens after a brief shower of rain that had transformed the stark landscape into something softer and less alien; the feelings this scene engendered were further enhanced when I came across a clear stream with a mass of wild roses cascading over it. I also noticed a strange plant pushing through the moist earth. It resembled a small spiky orange but had no leaves, and it brought to mind the brilliant flowers that suddenly appear in the African bush immediately after the pre-rain bushfires. Birds also enjoyed the moist atmosphere. We saw iridescent sun birds, brilliant bee-eaters, turquoise, black and red Abyssinian rollers and a variety of glossy starlings. After two days of this lotus eating and the usual protracted farewells, we pushed on towards Taiz.

Taiz

As we approached this city, the road surface improved, and avenues of flowering gums and acacia trees grew on either side. Suddenly, for the first time since arriving in Yemen, I got the impression of some community spirit. The town itself has cleaner streets, the souk has wide, well-swept alleyways, and the traffic is slightly less chaotic and more English is spoken.

The clinic in Taiz has been operating for twenty years and is now functioning well without expatriate staff. This is, of course, the aim of all foreign aid projects. The Abs Project plan envisages expatriate involvement for ten years. That evening we toured the souk on foot, enjoyed a meal together and compared our nursing experiences. We all agreed it had been the best day of our trip so far.

Mocha

On our way out of Taiz and on to Mocha – this is pure-desert scenery – we passed through a perfect, picture-book oasis of running water, green grass and palm trees. Further on, irrigated maize and sorghum fields created brilliant green patches in the golden sandy landscape where herds of camels roamed nibbling on bushes. As we approached Mocha on a good road we noticed a huge black cloud, and then a great wind enveloped us in a dust storm through which we could vaguely discern piles of rubble. This dust storm operated right up to the seashore beside which was the hospital, and it blew around and into the building creating drifts and ridges of sand throughout it.

Here we met a beautiful young French nurse, her local counterpart and several women who are being trained as local birth attendants. They all seemed to be cheerful and cooperative. Later on, in the counterpart's house, a good meal was provided for twenty people. There was no problem over chairs, as a circular mat was laid on the floor around which we all sat. Children were called to sit beside the adults who made sure they had enough to eat. There was no conversation or nonsense from the children. Everyone ate silently and earnestly. Anything left was given to the dogs. During the meal the French girl was not allowed to do anything. She just lay down like Cleopatra, was massaged, made much of and fed tasty morsels! I found this fascinating and wondered if I could emulate her in Abs! After this repast, the ladies put on tinsel dresses and sweet-smelling jasmine necklaces and earrings before going off to a wedding party.

In order to find our sleeping places at the French girl's flat we had to negotiate streets of ruined buildings, as well as sand dunes. As we turned off into a narrower, darker alleyway of low dwellings with filthy drapes hanging at small windows, I suddenly thought of *Beau Geste,* and this was reinforced when we turned up steep, sandy stone stairs and stepped onto an open roof space with castellated embrasures at each corner. The whole place was sand-encrusted, with broken doors and crumbling walls. The toilet was a black hole in a floor which sloped to the outside wall to enable excreta to run off through a gap onto the road below.

After a walk on a black beach – where an ancient man operated his fish nets from a raft of palm trees lashed together – we enjoyed a cold Heineken beer back at the house. My friends cooked and ate a sandy tomato omelet eaten straight from the pan. I had bread and Marmite and slept on the roof in my bag under a brilliant full moon. In the morning I was pleased to find enough to eat from my sack because everything in the kitchen was covered in sand; the unwashed omelet pan was a most unappetizing sight.

Although Mocha appeared to be a filthy, decaying area – and must have been fine when coffee was exported – it was not depressing, at least as far as the clinic was concerned. The women there showed confidence and satisfaction in the work they were doing or being trained for. I couldn't help being curious about the lovely, happy-looking French girl in this incongruous setting and her petted position among the clinic ladies until I was told that she was about to go to France to be married to an equally beautiful young French doctor who had been at Mocha for a short while – Yemeni ladies adore brides and weddings.

We had a very hot journey north to Zabeed the next morning and I was too exhausted to walk around another dusty clinic or look at ancient buildings. By now I was tired of ruins, however beautiful or historic. We pushed on to Hodeidah where we enjoyed pints of tea within the cool comfort of the Ambassador Hotel. But we spent the night in someone's cockroach-infested flat; at least twenty of them were floating in the toilet bowl in the morning.

In Hodeidah we parted company, the others going on to the mountain project while I joined the crowd at the taxi-pool depot looking for a seat to Abs. Taxis take at least eight passengers and do not leave until they have an economic load. At the cafe stop the driver was charming to me, giving me food from his plate, paying for it and then taking me right up to the clinic doors in Abs. I have always enjoyed my lone excursions, and here I found I was able to use the little Arabic I had learnt without inhibition. In our compound the trees had grown well, there was a lot of mail and I was pleased to sleep outside in the moonlight and under my net. Abs looked fine after Mocha!

Love, Mum

Six

Letters from Sana'a: June 1984

2 June

Dearest Suzanne and Dennis,

I do hope your business venture is going along alright. I look forward to hearing about it. I suppose you won't be in a position to travel around as you did before, at least not yet. I often think of you and your comfortable home. If you could see me here! But I must say the house we have just moved into is much better – it's very nice by any standards, but it gets very crowded at times.

Three new people have joined us, and it is good not to be 'the new ones' anymore and to be able to show others around and use the little Arabic one has. It sounds great to those who know none! I made a big effort to have the house looking decent for their arrival, to explain how things work, and to have food in the house. We are only two minutes from a market anyway, but the new folks don't know that. Fiona and I remember how abandoned we felt on arrival – I remember we even had to go out immediately and buy our own milk and bread.

At the moment I sleep in a corner of a long, airy room which has lots of windows topped by crescents of colored glass. From here, I look down onto a large orchard and garden that is surrounded by the traditional

Yemeni houses. A neighbor keeps about eight sheep in a walled enclosure against her house. Every morning at six she goes to the garden, cuts fodder for the animals and lets them out of their pen into the yard. This week she has been making large round pancakes of their manure which she leaves to dry for use as fuel.

The language course goes on until the end of July, so I will have been here six months out of twelve before actually doing any work! I am hoping to have a ten- to fourteen-day holiday in early October, as well as going to the UK in December for two weeks. I may visit Egypt in October and go on the Nile.

To go back to the house I am currently living in: it being Ramadan now, very little work can be done on projects. Nearly all our people pile into Sana'a for unspecified lengths of time. Tonight we will have about fourteen sleeping here – all on mattresses on the floor. My room will have to be shared – something I don't like – but at least the room is large. There are some pleasant things about living in a community; there is always someone to talk to or something happening, but I do find it quite exhausting. I have had a really bad chest cold for three weeks, and was obliged to take antibiotics when it threatened to be bronchitis, but thereafter it soon cleared up.

Ramadan started on 31 May. Days are quiet; nights are extremely noisy. Because people are hungry in the daytime they rest or sleep (those who can). Some house-repair work is going on around here at night, which involves hammering and sawing, on top of which we hear howling dogs and cat-fights, the call to prayer, and the odd gun going off. Maybe I'll get used to it – but I plan to take a trip away next June!

One can get an incredible selection of fancy fabrics here, such as flocked, embroidered velvets, star-spangled voiles and silks. Eyelet-embroidered petticoats are popular, and I bought a length yesterday. It's rather nice, in cotton, but it comes in all sorts of silks and combinations of colors. Not the sort of material one would use at home, but fun. I've just made some pants out of black silk decorated with gold lurex spots, and I have bought a remnant of dark-navy velvet, thickly encrusted with gold, yellow and bronze, as well as a gorgeous length of navy blue stuff that has fine lines of iridescent green/pink running lengthways; it shimmers beautifully. I am making a collection of small amounts of fabulous fabrics for Sarah and Joanna [Jean's grandchildren]. I shall also get them each a pair of the black-satin traditional trousers that are baggy around the bottom and fitting over the leg. The bottom six inches are encrusted with rich embroidery. These trousers are made for children as well as adults.

Will finish now. I am sharing a table with a new girl for Abs; she is around twenty-nine, very nice, and we seem to get along well. Five of us are attending the Arabic course together.

I hope you have a good birthday. I can't send a card as there are none here.

Love, Mum

22 June

Dear Family,

I am still in Sana'a, attending the language school and having a very pleasant time, if you discount the real pain involved in learning Arabic. The hours are 9:00 a.m. to 2:00 p.m., six days a week, with cultural lectures in the afternoons. We're in small classes – all in Arabic, which needs continuous concentration. Last week one of our activities included telling the class (four of us) a story – not long, of course. The others had to remember what was said because the storyteller then asked the others questions on their story.

On Saturday last, several of us went to the British Embassy for a party to celebrate the Queen's birthday. It was held in the gardens which were lit up at nightfall and looked pretty. Unfortunately, the music was canned – not what I am used to. In Germany we would have had the regimental band! It reminded me of Government House cocktail parties in Seychelles on the lawn above Victoria Harbor. The setting here is not so beautiful but the people attending were more friendly and pleasant than in colonial times. I enjoyed myself enormously: talked with the Czech Ambassador's wife about Kaska and Prague; then to an Indian diplomat and his doctor wife about their attitudes to British rule in India, both of whom had been educated in mission schools and said that, although they hated the way the British had kept aloof from Indians in those days, they felt they would not have had such a good education without the British background. I then talked at length to a Somali doctor in WHO [World Health Organization] – who had surprisingly accommodating views on South Africa – a gold-braid-covered American officer, a drunken British electrical engineer from a big power station near Hodeidah, and then various British people I already knew.

At the end of this week we will have done five weeks of the course and we will have a week's holiday to the north of Sana'a. I am planning to travel to Sada'a, which is near the Saudi border. It is a wild place, even more ancient than Sana'a. The population don't have much to do with central government. They still hanker after the 'good old days' before the Revolution in the 1960s. Saudi Arabia keeps the pot boiling up there. They don't want North Yemen too united or they might turn towards the other half of the country which is communist. Yemen is a divided country because of the British presence in Aden – before that it was one country but always at tribal war. It could hardly have been called a well-defined state, more a collection of warring tribes.

25 June

As part of our cultural activities, we went to the cinema last night with our teachers. One of them, Ismael, belongs to a small aristocratic sect (Shia) who claim they are directly descended from the only righteous heir to Muhammad – apparently the other sects also believe this. Ismael's father was killed in the civil war of the 1960s. He had a high position in pre-revolutionary society here. But they seem to be comfortably off under the Republic. I visited his mother and her friends one evening recently. Social intercourse is strictly segregated: the men have a separate *muffrage*, more beautiful and elaborate than the women's. The time for visiting during Ramadan is 9:00 p.m. (after the fast has been broken), and although we could not join in much conversation we felt at ease; we were given hot sweet tea, cold sweet drinks, nuts (toasted sunflower seeds), sweet cakes, and were offered a pull on the hubble-bubble pipe as well as choice leaves of khat to chew. We were there for two hours. Neighbors came in for half an hour – news and gossip were exchanged. One young woman (unmarried) was embroidering a beautiful wide belt for her future husband. About halfway through the proceedings, our teacher came home, gorgeously attired in his tribal costume: a long white garment, beautiful belt, carved jambia and immaculate turban. He looked like Sheikh Yamani! Fiona has developed a 'pash' for him and is totally frustrated because Ismael is uninterested in all her efforts to get his attention. I am sure he views us as pretty low creatures! They are very proud and sure of themselves, and are uncorrupted by western culture as yet.

Back to the trip to the local cinema. The building is a huge barn of a place with side entrances marked 'Balcony' and so on, like a London theater. The large floor was bare concrete, and for seating we had hard non-flammable bucket seats. Everyone smoked in spite of notices not to. We were an object of curiosity, being the only women in the place.

The usher was a scruffy individual with one cheek bulging with khat, eyes staring and glassy, and tousled hair. He carried a large stick under his arm with which he showed us our seats. He watched everyone; some youngsters tried to sit in the more expensive seats. When they wouldn't move for him, a soldier with a fairly lethal-looking gun was called to deal with the situation. When any of the audience moved too much or in any way blocked the view of the chaps behind, they would get a gun-tap on their head in no uncertain manner. The 'choc-ices and cigarette' types just had bottles of water stuck under their arms, cigarette packets in their pockets, and were also chewing khat and appeared to be fairly filthy!

During the performance (an Indian romance of heroism with Arabic subtitles) the audience clapped, cheered and shouted at each other, although the sound was loud enough to drown all this activity. Ismael sat himself securely among the men of our group, totally frustrating Fiona, who left in the middle of the film because the smoking was annoying her. The whole affair was pleasantly amusing – the film, the atmosphere, the antics of my friend. I stayed until the bitter end at 11:30 p.m. We all had tea in a barn of a cafe adjoining the cinema before taking a taxi home. The next installment of this letter will be after my trip to Sada'a.

After Sada 'a

I went to Sada'a on Saturday 30 June by group taxi. This means the taxi waits until the required number of passengers arrive. We waited one and a half hours and were still one short. So we all paid extra to make up for that. The cost was around eleven pounds for 150 miles. The good road to Sada'a – due north from Sana'a – goes through wild and desolate country of rocky, crumbling, dun-colored mountains. There is no terracing or signs of cultivation. It is an area subjected to tribal fighting and feuds.

We stayed in a reasonable hotel – ten pounds a night for bed and bathroom – but the food was very poor. It was the national religious holiday after Ramadan, and practically all the shops were closed. However, we were able to walk around the old city on top of the city walls – these were still almost intact, despite being built around the tenth century – and view the pretty and unique houses built of mud and straw centuries ago. That building technique is still used now. I found a book called *The Builders of Yemen*, which has wonderful descriptions of Sada'a, particularly its architecture. Some of these houses have such a smooth pearly finish. They are quite tall and slightly tapered with castellated tops, often painted white. Looking away from the city you see a forbidding barren landscape, surrounded by a ring of desolate mountains about five to ten miles distant.

One area just outside the city walls is an old burial ground. It has several mausoleums falling apart, adding to the ancient and desolate air one feels there. The people are charming as long as you are not having a quarrel over property. This area is more or less autonomous, and murders are paid for in blood money. When money is paid to the aggrieved party, the murderers are released. The money is not always sufficient so further killing is required!

One morning we walked in villages and fields north of the city towards a large fortress sitting on the edge of cliffs. Here, more pretty houses surrounded by their own mud walls looked just like medieval manor houses. Each one had its own water pump and irrigation to surrounding fields. The numerous vineyards behind vine-covered mud walls presented a scene of brilliant green against the brown unwatered area outside.

One of the most charming interludes of my stay in this area was when a man and his wife and children invited us to share their picnic of hot sweet tea and sour bread. They were under a tree, watching a herd of sheep and pretty young lambs. I had just thought to myself what a perfect picture it would make when the man waved us over. He spread out a long shirt for me to sit on. We stayed with them at least an hour, during which time he sent his heavily veiled and silent wife off. She came back with a bowl of grapes from their vines. Eventually we got a picture but the sheep had wandered off by then. Just as we were leaving I realized there was a baby in a sling hung on a branch of the tree! Two boys of eight and ten were starting to learn English at school.

We visited the modern American hospital in Sada'a – which sits in splendid isolation from Yemeni life – and had a good lunch there, which we much appreciated. As I said earlier, only a few small shops were open. One sold Coke, matches and cigarettes, tiny tins of cheese, biscuits, cheap belts, and a whole variety of inexpensive goods; here, I espied, right at the back, a beautiful, long, bottle-green velvet, mandarin-style coat, encrusted with gold braid, colored sequins, glass and pearls. I couldn't believe it! I asked the shop-keeper about it – yes, I could have it for 300 rials (about forty pounds). I bought it immediately and am thrilled with it. I might wear it here – goodness knows where else – it is just gorgeous to look at!

We took a taxi back to Sana'a. As I still had a few days' holiday before recommencing the language course I went to an American party on 4 July. It was on someone's roof top. I was too tired to stay long but I began to get a good feeling of belonging to these groups of volunteers. I know many of them now and they call out, 'Hi Jean,' which feels rather nice.

Another day I went to the top of the highest mountain in this part of the world – Jabal an Nabi Shu'ayb – which has an altitude of just over 12,000 feet. This is not as heroic as it sounds as you can drive most of the way. The last three miles is up a very rough path comprising lots of different colored rocks. On top of the mountain there is a small mosque and an old Turkish fort. I saw very few birds up there – only some griffon vultures and one large soaring bird that looked white underneath but I didn't get a good look.

I started school again on Saturday. What a painful business it is. I am with a bright group and have difficulty keeping up. I have to concentrate all the five hours to catch the sounds and try to make sense of them. But our teachers speak hardly any English and have to act out words for us to find their meaning.

The Abs Project has bought a new car – a Toyota Land Cruiser. It was smuggled into Yemen from Saudi across the Empty Quarter, and is hidden in a garden. It is supposed to be at a customs post on the border waiting for formalities. It cost around 1,500 pounds, and would be almost double that with tax if imported properly. I don't quite understand how the smuggling works. Of course the majority of cars here are driven by people with no license or insurance, but even so, most cars wear registration plates!

Great excitement: two days ago it was announced that oil has been found here, near Marib. The wife of the Texan in charge of the drilling attends Arabic lessons with us. She was so excited and pleased for her husband, but many people think it will destabilize this area even further. Saudi is angry (we are told); they don't want North Yemen to be independent of them. This oil find is on the edge of the Empty Quarter and the border between Yemen and Saudi there is ill-defined.

Two nights ago, Fiona said she would love to have a drink – we rarely see alcohol here, of course – and would I go to Taj Sheba Hotel with her? We got there around 8:30 p.m. It is very nice – not as plastic or unreal as the Sheraton – and has beautiful rugs, brass lamps, colored windows and space, not to mention wonderful service. We had a bottle of Mateus Rosé and some attractive Chinese hors d'oeuvres, stayed until 11:00 p.m. and saw a few acquaintances. Our meal set us back thirty pounds for two but it was worth every penny. We were celebrating the fact we had been here five months.

You will all be pleased to hear that I actually start work in less than three weeks' time at Abs, but the address remains the same. My next long letter will be in a few months' time, which should contain sterner stuff! I plan to spend three weeks with Katherine in England at Xmas.

Love, Mum

Seven

SETTLING IN – SANA'A, YEMEN: JULY 1984

Dear Family,

It is now the end of July and since my last letter I have spent three weeks in Abs, visited the mountain project and completed the language school in Sana'a. In Abs I was taken to meet the gas merchant and the water carrier and their families; I have also had some driving practice in preparation for the test in Sana'a. I spent mornings in the clinic learning to read and write the children's names and the medicines we prescribe in Arabic and answering midwifery calls. Until now women have relied on their village midwives for help at delivery; but now they have heard about the foreign women in Abs, so when the labor is not progressing normally they decide to come along and see what we have to offer. If we think a woman can deliver normally she either goes home or stays in our tiny delivery room in the clinic; otherwise she must be persuaded to go on to the hospital in Hodeidah. There are absolutely no facilities for surgery here in the clinic, although the Sudanese staff treat many minor cuts, gashes, burns, etc. Under the circumstances – with the scarcity of water and no sterilizing facilities – I wondered how this was done. It appears the relatives are sent to one of the many pharmacies in the village to buy pre-packed dressings, disposable forceps, syringes, and a supply of intravenous saline for cleaning the wound!

One day, while exploring the village, I almost fell over a camel that was sitting down in the narrow alleyway. He had a woven string muzzle over his nose and mouth through which someone fed him small quantities of grass from a nearby pile. I am told the muzzle stops the beast over-eating, although I imagined it also stopped him from biting the vulnerable legs of passers-by.

A family group of ladies invited us one evening into their compound where we sat on beds they had arranged in a companionable semicircle. Older children sat on mats in the center eating pumpkin seeds, drinking Coke, or were sent on errands. The very young children were put in cotton slings that were suspended under the beds in such a way that the women could rock them gently as they enjoyed the social evening. Under each sling was placed a container for urine. Outside the circle of beds, sheep, goats and two cows lay peacefully chewing. We ourselves were fed salty seeds, hot sweet tea or Coke and were decorated with jasmine flowers. Our pretty hostesses wore long tinselly nylon dresses and head coverings and looked beautiful in the moonlight.

One evening a crowd of women and children poured into our yard, and rushed around looking in all our rooms before settling down on the verandah to wait for a drink and sunflower seeds. On such occasions, the husks are scattered on the floor and there is copious spitting.

Most of the time I was in Abs the weather was awful due to thick dust storms and extreme heat. We have no fans and in any case the electricity comes on, unreliably, from 6:30 p.m. to 10:00 p.m. I had several attacks of sinusitis and stomach gripes. Friday is our designated day off when some of us go to Hodeidah by bus or project car, where, if one is lucky, well-heeled expatriates in luxurious houses may invite one in. On entering such homes, a childish old English ditty comes into my head, 'Hark, hark the dogs do bark, the beggars are coming to town, some in rags, some in bags and some in velvet gowns.'

On my way back to Sana'a I was taken to the mountain project. The rough road to it went up and up unceasingly amongst the sharp-edged mountains on which houses were perilously perched. The team up there live in part of an old Turkish fort where they have made themselves relatively comfortable. I was given a charming white-washed, cell-like room with unglazed embrasures for windows. In the night a small furry animal with a long striped tail came in to catch moths. During this visit I met a most unlikely character – a Scot who had sold his sausage factory in Fife and then taken a job here organizing abattoirs. He was a keen photographer and naturalist.

Water is brought up the hill every day by donkey and then carried into the house. Of course, we had to use it sparingly. As usual, the bathroom – or *hamaam* – intrigued me. The lavatory had a neat little seat over a projection in the thick walls; this jutted out away from the wall, allowing the excreta to fall down a huge precipice – an interesting experience.

Next morning we breakfasted on a small walled roof patch and enjoyed splendid views over the serried mountain ranges. The group here have recruited and set up a training course for health workers who will return to their villages, where, hopefully, they will practice what they have learned. Here I again met my traveling companion from London, Fiona. While taking a walk and exchanging experiences we saw a poor little donkey with his hind strap pulled so tight it had cut into his upper back leg. It was bleeding. Even so he was being beaten to go faster. The people here seem utterly indifferent to the welfare of donkeys, dogs and cats.

Early one morning I was put in a taxi for the long journey to Sana'a, which entailed following the long rough track to the desert and then up the escarpment. I arrived in the evening to find we had 'moved house' – a great improvement! I share a room with Fiona when we are in town. My bed position looks out over a large walled garden where several sheep are also kept. I like that.

My driving test was successfully taken. It was important for me to have success in something. I seem not to be finding a useful niche as I always have in other situations. The *mudeer* (the boss) at the driving center reminded me of Azdak, the judge in *The Caucasian Chalk Circle*, being a small man with a crumpled face who had us all in his power.

Torrential rain has fallen making the streets a sea of mud. Now I know why I was told to bring wellies [rubber boots]! One day, on my way to our house along a mud- and filth-logged alley, I was intrigued to see a few small children with sticks driving a pack of decrepit cats. It looked like a grotesque circus act, with the cats running slowly with their tails down as lions do with their tamers.

I helped set up our new house by cleaning, cooking and curtain-making. I visited city clinics and the well-known Save the Children clinic in Rowdha. During my city travels we visited the fish souk to find some good-quality fresh fish. I bought a red snapper and made bouillabaisse à les Seychelles. The ladies who own the garden invited us to their house. When not occupied with their farming chores they travel extensively, mainly to East Germany, Egypt, and China where a sister lives.

The Language School: 28 July

The language school has been endured; it has been a mixed blessing. I started full of enthusiasm and good intentions but, gradually, as it appeared that I learned or remembered very little, I became depressed. Many times on my way to school I felt like a child who plays truant, but being older I knew it was not in my best interests to do so! Our teachers were Yemeni university students, most of whom knew no English, so I had no way of asking questions. I believe this is the modern method of teaching foreign languages but I find it horribly intimidating. Once I have lost my way in the lesson I am unable to catch up as one could in French or German where there would be some familiar sound to latch onto. Arabic is completely different. Unfortunately, I have come away with negative feelings about my ability with the language. Our teachers were all charming and friendly, and one or two caused heartache to several students, specially the beautiful Sabri and the aristocratic Ibrahim! Even I could gaze on them in appreciation!

The students – Dutch, American, Swiss, French and ourselves – were sixteen in number divided between four classrooms. School hours were six days a week from 8:00 a.m. to 2:00 p.m., after which, apart from homework, I cooked, cleaned and shopped for the house with others and joined in most of the expeditions and social activities within our group and with the teachers.

In the early optimistic phase of my school life the weather was quite lovely. I woke to hear birds chirping, cocks crowing, the garden being watered by opening the irrigation channels, and sheep being let out of their pens and talked to by their young lady keepers. The morning sun on this biblical scene often made me wish I was camping in the desert near Rada, but fantastic storm clouds usually built up, and in order to appreciate the unusually clear air, blue sky and strange cloud formations, we would take our tea onto a small roof space. Each morning we walked about a mile to school through the Al Hamd Palace Hotel garden with its little streams of running water, patches of vegetables and fruit trees. Sometimes we were saddened to see a poor little donkey dragging about with a broken leg. Apart from the pleasures of the garden on our way to school, we traversed several narrow alleys that are being excavated for a new sewage system by Chinese engineers.

One day I came across two respectable ladies wearing the elegant, long black dresses and head and face covers with only their eyes and hands exposed. They appeared to be deep in conversation but as I drew nearer I noticed a couple of cats doing what cats usually do out of sight! The ladies couldn't resist casting glances at the cats' randy behavior. I was amused by the total picture, but being bare-faced and foreign I didn't think it seemly to join the audience. I couldn't deny prurient curiosity whereas the veiled ladies could maintain they had never seen the cats. The black dresses many women wear here are most elegant, being made of heavy crepe that hangs, drapes and flows becomingly as they walk. Many wear black gloves and leave a trace of perfume in the air – this and the crackle of taffeta under skirts all add to their glamour.

In addition to those taking the language course, our house saw a constant stream of visitors who found corners to sleep in. This caused the water cistern to run dry but most of us did our best to keep the bathroom and kitchen clean. Inevitably, there were one or two who evaded such tasks. Nevertheless, we had a lot of fun, and birthdays and departures would be occasions for a feast followed by the talented fooling around dancing or singing their set pieces. During the last month of term the party season came into full swing. We invited the teachers to our house for lunch. They stayed late into the evening but not before several other local friends had wandered in, eaten up the leftovers and joined in the rather serious conversation – mainly about local history and politics.

A Swiss pupil in our school gave a more sophisticated party in her apartment, where food was brought in by caterers, and wine and champagne flowed generously. One of our women gave a splendidly slinky, seductive dancing display, a ploy I imagine to get those handsome chaps on the floor. Soon we were all cavorting about making quite a noise, and our hosts introduced juggling and card tricks in order to quieten us down before we emerged onto the street where larking about would lead to police probing.

The teachers reciprocated by throwing an evening party in the school building that happened to fall on my birthday (20 July). During the evening they made a circle with me in the center and each one danced with me. I thought that very civil of them considering my advanced years, but I think they feel more at ease with older women. I wore the gorgeous, long dark-green velvet, mandarin-collared coat that I had bought in Sada'a. One of the Dutch contingent gave a hilarious mimicry of an Indian fakir that had us all in stitches.

We are now into the final weeks of school and I have not yet told of our pleasant daily breakfast routine. As far as I am concerned, the best moment of the day is at 10:00 a.m. when we all troop off to a nearby cafe to sit on rickety folding chairs at clean covered tables, set up on the narrow pavement of a busy highway, to breakfast on hot bean stew, sweet tea and delicious flatbread. The bread is brought hot from ovens which resemble the old farmhouse kitchen 'copper' in which certain items of laundry were boiled or pig potatoes cooked. Here, a fire burns underneath the ovens and flattened dough is pressed against the hot linings to cook. We are so hungry and happy to be released from the classroom that we don't notice the cacophonous traffic. Yemeni city drivers are always in a hurry, sitting forward over their steering wheels on the lookout for the slightest chance to overtake. At the traffic lights they halt reluctantly. As the red light changes all horns and hooters are put into operation.

In spite of my stomach problems I am always hungry. Eating is probably the only cozy pleasure available – and Yemen with its exciting landscapes, brilliant inhabitants, raucous, rough and unpredictable village and city scenes is anything but cozy. Having said that, one is at times reminded of childhood biblical stories; the God-like bearded old men in long white gowns, the camel trains, laden donkeys, water carriers, narrow streets and of course the desert all create an ambience of timelessness to which one can relate. It compensates in some way for the ugliness brought about by modern technology.

Before the end of term we made several forays into the souk, especially in the late evenings during Ramadan. One visit was particularly memorable because it was not crowded, and we had time to look up at the pretty houses whose colored-glass windows shone like jewels under the half-moon in the sky. I bought gifts of Cashmere cushion covers and shawls, and as we wandered at will, we came across alleyways that led along to cave-like workshops, brilliantly lit by blow lamps, blacksmiths' forges and Primus stoves. Men stripped to the waist hammered, soldered and fashioned jambias, nails, locks, buckets and all manner of necessary objects. I was amazed at their ingenuity and was reminded of certain artists' fascination with, and depiction of, the Industrial Revolution.

On our last day off we planned another picnic into the mountains, and we were to leave at 9:00 a.m. The keen ones – such as myself – got up early in order to be ready on time. Others – who were not so keen but did not wish to be left behind – were not ready. One came without her passport, sweater or hiking boots. Just before reaching the village at the foot of the hill we had a puncture. Those not involved in wheel-changing walked on and got a lift in a lorry part-way up. Most mountains here have a road or track all the way to the top where there will be either an old Turkish fort or a mosque. This mountain – like others we have visited – was exquisite, being remote, wild and silent apart from a shepherd-ess whistling to her flock. Growing among the rocks were little round tufty plants like pin-cushions, dotted with gentian-blue, nine-petaled flowers just showing through their brownish-red foliage. Other plants had mauve, pink, purple and yellow flowers. At one corner of this flat-topped hill perched in precarious fashion an old fort, and beside it a tiny mosque had candles burning within. A woman's dress had been left to dry on a rail nearby. We sat outside awhile admiring the fantastic views reminiscent of the Grand Canyon – but without the crowds. On our way down we met the puncture-repair team who were carrying the picnic which we shared. They went on to the top and we all met at the car at 5:00 p.m. Our reluctant fellow traveler had spent the day in the village with our Yemeni girlfriend and teacher.

The language course ended without examinations or prize giving. We were soon to be dispersed. Playtime was over and I have still to write my first six-month report.

Love, Mum

Eight

WORK BEGINS IN ABS: AUGUST 1984

Dear Family,

I came to Abs ten days ago – actually to start work, at last! I am quite glad to have been obliged to fool around in Sana'a for six months before coming to this gruesome hole!

My first few days here began with feelings of intense loneliness and some anxiety, reinforced by the threatening storm clouds that gathered daily. But all we got was thick dust clouds and desolation. In an effort to counteract this I put my energies into an attempt to improve my immediate surroundings. I took on the task of watering the newly planted trees with used water from the kitchen, put bougainvillea cuttings and a few simple plants around my verandah posts – and they flourished for two weeks, giving me great pleasure. But then the plasterers arrived to decorate our newly constructed huts, and this was accomplished by throwing handfuls of wet plaster at the walls where some stuck to be smoothed over, but the rest fell down around the building completely covering my plants. I couldn't believe my eyes, not just at the destruction of my feeble attempts at gardening but also over the sheer ham-fisted and wasteful method of plastering.

My next effort involved finding my way to the souk where, using my hard-won and sparse Arabic, I bought rice, onions, tomatoes and potatoes and came across the sesame mill, activated by a camel walking in continuous circles. The miller sells a good selection of seeds, pulses and grains and I love going there. When the camel isn't working he seems to spend his time sitting down by his master who feeds him sorghum stalks through a string muzzle. At this same spot one day I saw a group of black-gowned women all wearing their conical, yellow straw hats, crouching around baskets of dried fish. A man riding a laden donkey passed through their midst, his feet almost touching the ground; at least six other donkeys were tethered in a row, standing patiently, first on one leg then on the other, their heads low, waiting for their rough task-masters. All this, together with the sesame mill, would have made a wonderful scene for an artist.

After these forays into the souk, I enjoy preparing a meal, although the kitchen is dark and hot at 105°F – and we have frequent water shortages. The stove works quite well on Calor gas. Refills are obtained by driving out to the gas dealer's house with empty cylinders – a heavy job. These basic activities give my life a feeling of ordinariness in an extraordinary setting.

As well as these little outings, I started going to the clinic almost immediately, but, because the midwifery project was not yet established, I worked in the sick children's room, although we had very few patients. We had to persuade the government doctors to send the children over to us for health information, weighing and immunizations. Most children are brought in with severe dehydration for which we supply the simple oral rehydration fluid. This requires constant spoon-feeding. We demonstrate how it is done and encourage them to stay an hour or two. Some find this treatment too simple or time-consuming and hope for a nice, big, expensive injection after which the baby will be well.

Ninety percent of the children we see are sick, under-weight, under-nourished, worm-infested and malaria-ridden. We see cases of open obvious TB every week. No one is too bothered. It's all the Will of Allah. Diet is very poor, especially since the country became open to foreign trade. Baby milks and bottles are responsible for so much illness and death here. Every day we have one or two severely dehydrated babies due to dirty bottle-feeding, diarrhea and vomiting. At least two died this week in the clinic.

Difficult midwifery cases arrive in a state of exhaustion and dehydration having traveled a long way in this intense heat. Yesterday we had one that brought back memories of some of the worst cases I had dealt with in Malawi. Of course, we have no facilities for surgery here and the doctors are awful. We are to have two young doctors from the UK join our group at the end of the year. It will be interesting to see how they cope with the situation.

I must clarify our position here so that you might understand what I am on about.

Abs was chosen as a suitable site for an experiment by our organization – to see if our presence here could improve medical practices. But we are seen as a threat to the Sudanese doctors and nurses and the local staff who charge patients for a service that should be free. However, Yemeni staff hardly ever get paid. It is assumed they are able to make enough money privately. Yet the government advertise their health service as free. We don't charge; we get our pay regularly and our well-being is assured. So you see it is a crazy illogical system. The government are unable to enforce their laws. We are tolerated in the clinic and Yemenis are very polite people, but resent us because of our attitudes. Our British organization is always questioning whether or not we should be here and if it is possible to realize any of their aims, the prime one being to try to get poor people to think they can do something to improve their lot in life. It does seem a remote hope here, given the religious and cultural atmosphere, and the fact that the people have been totally seduced by the international drug companies. Sometimes I think our group are a bit arrogant. I think people can only learn things through experience, not by us telling them it is so.

We come back from the clinic at 1:00 p.m. every day, have lunch and then go to our rooms, shut the doors and have the fan on until 4:00 p.m. Today (as with every day when I come out), I looked at the desolate scene and asked myself why the hell I am here! I see the usual thick dust storm, the yard littered with plastic bags and paper blown in from rubbish dumps outside. In fact, Abs looks like a huge desolate rubbish dump. I didn't feel too good today so went to the kitchen and swept out half a bucket of dirt and sand, and cleaned the top of the cooker. I then cleared up the yard – more stone clearance. I showered – we have to carry water by bucket to a tank aloft as the pump was broken two months ago. I'll stay as long as I feel fit and can laugh! And so far I am very well: no headaches; no pain in my hip.

The clinic is a collection of cement-block rooms in a desolate court-yard. The iron-grille gates are broken, leaving just a small space to enter. It is just the right height to smash one's head on. Facing you is a broken-down ambulance; to the right a wheel-less Land Rover lies at an angle. In one corner is the water pipe, which leaks all day, so there is a muddy hole around it. There is no running water but our cleaning lady Ayesha has a washing machine and carries water by bucket to the machine.

I have already mentioned Ayesha, our resident witch. She knows how to control the women who are excessively modest. When they come in with gynecological problems they are terrified of their bodies being touched or seen. I've had to do internal examinations and catheteriza-tions etc. for the male doctors. Ayesha is invaluable in these situations. There is no nonsense with her around. With a few strong words, she has the woman lying down in position pretty smartly! There is also an ancient chap around here – another cleaner I believe – who shakes hands all around every morning.

Taxis arrive at the clinic packed with sick families. One gets the impression that the village headman waits until there are enough sick people to warrant the journey. At the clinic he will shepherd them into the room, clutching the papers issued at the entrance gate. Each paper has a child's name on it, and many have the same name, usually con-nected with The Prophet. The headman helps us by identifying each child and getting them in an orderly line. While they are here we encour-age them to have the children immunized, and the pregnant women to take iron tablets; we also introduce the idea of family planning.

We've had a spate of septic infected scalps, especially in little girls who wear tight-fitting bonnets of thick nylon velvet – in this heat, and no water for washing. I long to take off the headgear and wash their heads, but that would be sacrilege. We see a few children with severe malnutrition, not necessarily because of poverty but because when the mother becomes pregnant again she ceases to breastfeed so the baby has to take pot luck. Only the lusty ones who will eat anything come through unscathed. We do our best to introduce the idea of early weaning using suitable foods from the family diet.

One of the Sudanese doctors resembles Idi Amin and he is most interested in midwifery cases – always ready to 'try' anything. One morning I found him, cigarette dangling from his mouth, about to do a high forceps delivery with the uterus in tonic contraction. I managed to persuade him through flattery and cajolery to send the patient to Hodeidah. But was I right to have done so? I only know I could not assist in such a dangerous procedure. We never hear the results of these transfers unless the woman happens to deliver normally en route. Then our resident Witch Doctor, Ayesha, comes roaring up to me, shaking her hennaed finger under my nose, to infer how foolish I had been. I remain unmoved and say how delighted I am that the patient was spared hospitalization.

When we are required in the clinic or in the village at night, we are alerted by a furious hammering on our large metal doors. We approach them with trepidation as one never knows what bizarre situation will be revealed. Usually the case is presented by several excited, anxious men shouting, 'Shaf'a Ha, Ayn'a Ha' (look at her, help her), at the same time pointing towards the Toyota truck where several little black-veiled heads are to be seen bobbing up and down. We see them next door in the clinic.

One evening a pretty young woman was brought to the door by two older women asking us if we would circumcise her as she was about to be married! Language prevented further investigation into the case but they offered us 'plenty of money.' We were of course unable and unwilling to help them.

The clinic at night is something to behold: the doctor, nurses and male relatives all sitting around comfortably chewing khat and smoking by the light of a hurricane lamp, while the female patient, usually waiting for catheterization, suffers quietly in a dark corner. If there is no water we send a relative out into the village to get some, from where I don't know, and the urine drains into used Shamlan drinking-water bottles.

A man with a donkey bite on his thigh was stitched up satisfactorily by using sterile intravenous saline to wash the wound and stitching material bought in a sterile pack from the local pharmacy. I was quite amazed – it seemed crazily expensive – but it is effective here when the alternative is going to Hodeidah by taxi. The patient recovered without complications. The affair of the donkey bite first came to my attention as I walked down the clinic verandah and noticed a trickle of blood slowly oozing out from under the closed door of the treatment room. I looked and listened but not a sound was to be heard. What went on in the treatment room was none of my business; nevertheless I was always curious and usually the door would be open and there would be plenty of noise. This time, the silence and the closed door seemed sinister and eerie to say the least. I felt somewhat affronted in that I was not taking part in this drama as I would have been in my hospital work in Malawi. Another eye-opener for me was how someone with extensive burns is treated here, always using the sterile packs and solution, without a sign of infection.

We often get invited to call on families we meet in the clinic, especially those accompanied by headmen. One afternoon we called on one such family. They own land, tractors, a Land Cruiser and trucks. A six-day-old baby had diarrhea and a raw bottom. The mother, very young with her first baby, had severely inverted nipples and couldn't suckle her baby who was being fed incorrect milk mixture from a filthy bottle. There was no water shortage in that situation. They have their own borehole and donkeys to carry it to the house. I went along with them on one journey, riding back on the donkey. Poverty was not the problem either – they didn't understand the importance of clean bottles and properly reconstituted milk powder. Bottles and baby food are readily available from the ubiquitous drug stores, but there are no easily understood instructions as to their use, or any stress on their misuse.

Another household we visit frequently in the village is that of our charming young clerk Hind in the children's room. She belongs to a highly respected family. Her father had been an imam and had encouraged Hind to become literate in Arabic and versed in its classical literature and poetry. She is obviously highly intelligent and attractive and is the mainstay of her widowed mother and extended family. We are most fortunate to have her services, and, coming from such an influential family, the health messages she carries from the clinic will be far more effective than anything we say.

About once a month we spend our day off in Hodeidah. I have been given the key to a flat we use there as a base, which is occupied by one of the few Roman Catholic priests in Yemen. He is a charming interesting person from Algeria who seems to lead a torturous, almost underground, existence in this xenophobic Islamic state. He is only tolerated because he ministers to the spiritual needs of the nuns who run institutions for handicapped people. While in Hodeidah I spend time with expatriates in their comfortable homes, going on bird-watching expeditions and playing bridge.

One of the most important activities for the midwives is to get to know and obtain the goodwill of the old established village midwives. The only way to do this is to call on them frequently, but language is a constraint. One can understand local people preferring these well-known old family friends to the foreigners who are not even Muslims – the foreigners who think people can help themselves, that neo-natal and maternal deaths can be reduced by self-help and don't have to be passively accepted. I have lost a lot of weight since arriving in Yemen – around 15 pounds and look a bit like a scarecrow. I have no hip pain or headaches, however!

I am told the weather will become less hot from now on. Hope to hear from you soon. I wish I was in your kitchen right now.

Love, Mum

PS We watched Sebastian Coe win a race at the Olympics last week at the transport cafe up the road from here.

Nine

BACK IN SANA'A: SEPTEMBER 1984

25 September

Dearest Katherine,

I was delighted to get your long letter about Italy. You had quite an adventure. I have only read your letter once earlier today as I arrived from Hodeidah in a state of exhaustion.

It is wonderful to be in Sana'a again. Lots of our group are here for a big meeting.

One really has some frightful situations here. Yesterday morning I was with a woman with obstructed labor. No way could she push the baby out – she needed a Caesarian operation. We can't do that in Abs as we have no anesthetic, no instruments, no sterilization, etc. She should have been taken to Hodeidah, but her family said they couldn't afford the taxi fare. They needed 100 to 150 pounds for that. So they took her home – to die I suppose, unless a miracle occurred. I felt terrible and useless. She pleaded with me to do something; our doctor wouldn't do anything for the above reasons. She was such a brave little woman. I wonder what did happen to her. Perhaps her husband was able to raise the money back in his village. I felt badly about it because I had that much money in my purse ready for these few days in Sana'a. I am feeling a real bad lot. I know one can't help financially every time, but one could try it once and see what happened. I may never get the chance to be big-hearted in that way again.

It was great to leave Abs for a while. Judy took me to the bus stop and waited with me for the bus to come. In Hodeidah I stayed with a Dutch girl who was on the language course with us. She keeps her flat beautiful and it was a treat to be there. She also had air conditioning for the night. We have had quite a lot of rain in Abs; the nights have been incredibly hot and humid although the days have been a bit cooler.

Abs is challenging and I sometimes wonder if I have taken on more than I can manage. Some days it's fine, then other days one feels totally inadequate because of the language difficulty.

Judy and I are starting an antenatal clinic on 2 October – twice a week to start with. Judy has arranged it all and found an intelligent local woman to be our clerk and counterpart. So we hope some women turn up when we set up shop. A lot depends on our success here. It is something I could do if I find I don't quickly improve in the language. Judy is good at it and has been here six months longer. She wants to move out to the villages next year to train village women.

What depresses us all is the language issue, the heat, the isolation. I suspect that if there weren't a language problem one might not mind the other things so much. It makes you feel useless, stupid and ineffective. I think there is a limit to how long you can go on feeling like that. You need some success. The lack of civilized comforts also plays into the picture. Our toilet is a hole in the ground and I am tired of splashing my legs with pee. We also have to be careful with water – and of course not all are. When living in a communal way, as we do here, the habits and peculiarities of one's housemates can quickly become irritating. It is easy to let little things get under one's skin in this difficult environment.

I have taken on the responsibility of buying the water. We have to see a guy who goes to the wadi and loads a tank with water and then pumps it into our tank. I also look after the gas cylinders for the stove and fridge, and have been left in charge of the safe where we keep our money. Someone left the gas burner on unlit for an hour two days ago! One of our housemates is very unhappy with lots of personal problems, which is why she came of course, to try to escape them. It is no good coming to such a place with serious personal problems.

We have no comfortable chairs and eat in discomfort. We are always eating cabbage salad – I am sick of it! I can't get the bloody BBC easily either – I almost smash my radio in frustration. So far most things in the garden have died. So you see there's not much to lift one's spirits. No mail, no telephone, no food comforts either – not even butter or margarine. In spite of all this I don't think I am unhappy. I get disconsolate and depressed for short periods. I need some affection so I am looking forward to Xmas so very much. Probably will leave here for the UK on 8 December and come for four weeks.

Lord of the Flies incident

Since my arrival here in February, something about our volunteer organization personnel made me think of the novel *Lord of the Flies* and I was wondering if I might become 'Piggy' – so far I haven't but I have seen people type-caste for that role. My intuition about our group has been reinforced these past two days because of Fiona's position. You may remember she was ill when we first arrived; we were also robbed and the language course was put on hold. The whole experience here has been shocking to her. She came with rose-tinted glasses. Everything was beautiful, but of course it was not. Her job description seems to have turned out to be a can of worms, according to her. She is unable to recover from shocks and disappointments easily. She is with a group of strident young women who drive Land Rovers anywhere and speak Arabic quite well – they have been here much longer.

Fiona failed her driving test. It seems that all was stacked against her. It seems that these last few weeks she has been thoroughly depressed, not eating and has a septic infection. At the same time, a social researcher who speaks Arabic has been with her group assessing work done by two others who have left now, but were unhappy and depressed all the time they were here. The researcher says that their work was more or less useless and they should have left or talked about it. Apparently, everyone knew how they felt but turned away from the problem. So, they decided to have this meeting yesterday to see if Fiona was another disaster in embryo stage. It appears they did decide so, and all fell on her with criticism of her weaknesses – just like Piggy! This went on for three hours and she said nothing in her defense. She then left the meeting and came up to the room we share and told me she was leaving. Her job didn't exist anymore. I comforted her as well as I could and we went out together later. But I was shocked and angry at this brutal method. I am not supposed to know what happened, but I have another source of back-door information. Someone else at that meeting was totally shocked and said it was like a pack of hounds onto a fox. And all these young women have degrees in social science or psychology!

Our group appears to be tightening up on language proficiency with no sympathy or encouragement for those of us who find it difficult. When I am with one who speaks it well, I am tongue-tied. If I am alone I can find something to say. Don't worry – at the first sign of me being the next Piggy I will be on the next plane home. I hope not to stay to be reduced to the state Fiona is in.

My job is somewhat better defined than hers. I am supposed to be training village women; instead, we are delivering babies and starting an antenatal clinic. We have not found any village women who want to know anything about our ideas. Judy wants to start going out to villages to stay for several weeks and try to impart some information, or at least learn how they feel. You need to be good at the language and have stamina to live in horrible conditions for that. It will take years for people here to see the benefits of women having knowledge. They are excluded from professions, and it is considered a disgrace to be a nurse, or work in the clinic with a bare face. It is really like Victorian society. One has to remind oneself what a short time ago that really was. We do have one local young woman in the children's clinic and have found another to help in the antenatal clinic. They are of course not interested in dirty jobs. They will write in the register and make out cards, talk to people. It's a start I suppose. They are insulted every day by patients in the clinic.

I go back to Abs on Saturday.

Love, Mum

Ten

Dear Family,

It was wonderfully refreshing to meet old friends and to feel relaxed amidst familiar surroundings in England for two weeks in December. Arriving back in Sana'a was like having a kick in the stomach, even though my friends and fellow workers were most welcoming. The shock comes from the realization of just what one gives up by being in such a country. The first time round everything is a novelty. The second time it is a reality. Other team members were rushing about purposefully, carrying files, attending meetings, reading reports, while I looked on like a bird in the wilderness, not yet ready to plunge in. I was attending meetings on our project when a clever, astute, young woman doctor of 'this and that' proclaimed the Abs Project to be worthy of further funding and gave some of us courage to continue. Amongst the difficulties in this type of work is the timescale in which one can see results – as each of us is only here for two years, any one individual cannot expect to see much progress.

Back in Abs it was cool enough to sleep indoors. I continued to help in the children's room three mornings a week and do home visiting for the midwifery project the other three mornings, as well as take my turn in answering emergency calls. You never know what situations will be found on such calls. We have a rule never to go out of the village in answer to a call, but you can never be sure where the patient is if not in the car or truck with the family. One afternoon an old headman we knew from his clinic visits asked me to go to see his wife. He assured me they lived 'just down the path,' so against my better judgment I went along with him. I wouldn't have gone if I had not known him. But of course 'just down the path' turned out to be several miles away. One could say I was hijacked. At the house I found the wife to be in early labor with no obvious difficulties apart from it being her twelfth pregnancy. I had problems in persuading the husband to take me back to Abs. He wanted me to stay there until she delivered, which she did, but three days later!

Another difficult call came from one of the souk families at 1:00 a.m. when I was conducted to a tarpaulin lean-to shack in total darkness. On a narrow string bed lay a very young girl having hysterics, surrounded by village ladies trying to soothe her. On the outer circles were many neighbors with children – there for the entertainment. I stood for a while clutching my bag, taking in the scene and telling myself that this was just where the best type of village worker would fall into her own. Because the ground was muddy I put my bag on the lap of one of the ladies who then made a space for me on one of the string beds arranged around the patient. I asked what was up. They said she had lots of backache, was very young and frightened and wouldn't I give her 'The Injection'. I said, 'Fine, but I must have a look at her to make sure she is properly in labor, if the baby is lying in the correct position.' They allowed me a brief feel of the abdomen through layers of clothing but no way would I be allowed to examine internally. I explained I could not give the injection without knowing the baby's position and if there was no disproportion, because the drug induces strong contractions which can be very dangerous. This did not interest them, and they politely handed me my bag, led me to the van and I was escorted home. I felt relieved.

All the village people know about Syntocinon. It contains a hormone called oxytocin that causes the uterus to contract. It is used to induce labor or strengthen labor contractions; it can also be used to control bleeding after childbirth. It can be bought by anyone in the pharmacies and we use it diluted in an intravenous drip – in order to give it slowly – and so we can stop it quickly, but they like it to be given directly into the muscles. They must have some disasters in remote villages because anyone with a modicum of knowledge will happily give injections – for a fee. This particular baby was born in the night. I didn't inquire if the injection had been used when I called on them the next morning.

Our new doctor is very popular and numbers in the children's room have increased enormously. It is pandemonium in there! Especially on the few occasions when our clerk does not come and then I attempt to register each child, sometimes fifty of them, in our register in Arabic, and make out cards on which we chart their weights, which is achieved by weighing mother and child together, then the mother separately. Added to this puzzle are the scales which are in roman numerals over which our doctor has affixed Arabic numbers. At the same time we have a young woman working with us as a counterpart. The room is about twelve foot square, and one has to swim through the crowds of relatives – sometimes three generations come along with each child, who arrives in our room with a scrap of paper on which his/her name has been hastily scrawled. I can't decipher most of them, so I apply a process of elimination and register those I can easily identify first, then consult with the relatives about the rest. When our doctor is away I take her place, treating those with relatively simple conditions, sending them along for immunizations while our helpers talk about diet and hygiene. Those with serious conditions are referred to the Sudanese doctors across the yard.

On one such a day we had sixty-six through our room, starting at 8:00 a.m. and finishing at 2:00 p.m. I just kept my head down and concentrated on the child in question, completely imprisoned by the ring of anxious relatives all peering down, hoping for a miracle, which was not likely to occur! Most of the children we see are stunted, malnourished, some *in extremis* with worms, malaria, anemia, chest infections, and septic skin conditions. These illnesses are not often due to poverty but to cultural attitudes towards women and children, their expendability, and the passive acceptance of the Will of Allah. Under these conditions one forgets the intense heat or one's thirst, and I feel I am back in Africa. But the thirst here is something I have never experienced before, unquenchable by plain water. I find a weak, fresh lemonade the most effective and if anyone drinks (always straight from the bottle) in company in Yemen, one is obliged to share it with them, not a habit I relish in a room of sick people.

I am available for midwifery in the clinic or to examine or catheterize female patients for the male Sudanese doctors. While conducting these procedures I am closely supervised by dear Ayesha, the cleaning lady. I have decided it is in our best interests to cultivate her and maybe influence her, and now I call her my sister and counterpart.

Our clients are fascinated by gadgets, specially the auroscope introduced by our doctor, down which she peers into ears to the silent amazement of the crowd. In order to liven up my home visiting in similar vein, I now bring along a small sling-type scale to weigh the babies and plot the results on cards I have with me. It is not such a splendid thing as the auroscope and they do not wholly trust the sling. I carry iron tablets around for pregnant women because in any house one enters, neighbors pour in, most of whom will be pregnant. At the same time I tell them about the various clinics we have at the hospital, especially the immunizations. These are done by a Yemeni team trained by the two Australians who started the project and are about to leave us. They will be hard to replace.

I have a few special friends in the village who are very kind to me. Sometimes when they see I am exhausted and feeling ill they clear a space on a bed so that I can rest awhile and be fed some hot sweet tea. In other homes I am invited to join the family meal, squatting round a circular mat on the ground which serves as a tablecloth. As we eat, the domestic animals crowd round the periphery hoping for scraps. One friend, who lives a half mile outside the village, insists on giving me eggs and bananas which I am sure her children should be eating.

They all decorate the interior of their houses with hundreds of brightly colored tin trays from China, purchased in the weekly souk; these souks are brought to the village by a group of travelers who move around the countryside living in rough tents and lean-to open sheds. There is a lot of illness and mortality amongst their children.

We paid another interesting visit to a village headman's family recently, about twenty miles north of Abs. As we arrived the women and children rushed out to welcome us, but then the men in our group were taken off to the men's room to chew khat, smoke the hookah and chat about local politics. We were led off with the women and children to sit on string beds, drink hot tea or *gish*. *Gish* is made from coffee-bean husks, cardamom, and ginger boiled together in a locally made, earthenware, narrow-necked pitcher that has a bunch of fine twigs stuck in the neck as a cork. It is an old women's drink and only I am offered it when socializing. It is served in small earthenware beakers. If you leave any in your beaker it is poured back into the pitcher to be brewed up for the next social event. I used to enjoy it until I realized what was going on! Later, bottles of Pepsi or bright red and orange sugary drinks were pressed on us, sent for by one of the older children as soon as we arrived. It seems that wherever one is in Yemen cold soda pop and bottled water are instantly available in the most unlikely places. We played with the children, went to the well with them to get water – which donkeys carried in pitchers in string slings on either side of them – and the small children came along for the ride.

At the well a diesel pump supplied water to irrigation channels that criss-crossed the adjacent land. Ownership of the pump and well gives our friend power over others in the neighborhood. I looked longingly at these green fields and the distant hills and had a fleeting desire to run away, to escape the shackles of my present life!

Women here are obsessed by gold. It is of course their bride price and they think I am a poor thing not to have been purchased by my husband. They examined my ruby ring but were unimpressed about its worth; they only value heavy lumps of gold. They looked in my mouth for gold and noticed my dental plate. They were absolutely thunder-struck by it. I had to take it out for them to examine and anyone else coming in had to have a demonstration. My bra was the next thing to be commented upon. I was almost stripped in their eagerness to see it! I didn't mind – these afternoon visits can be a bit boring with such limited language skills. I couldn't help thinking that a glass eye or a wooden leg would be a godsend on these occasions.

Bird watching in Yemen

One of my great pleasures here is bird watching and this I do mainly with expatriate friends in Hodeidah. From them I learned of the splen-did potential for seeing a great variety of birdlife at the local sewage works. I accompanied this group one weekend to Taiz when I was already suffering from sinusitis but no worse than on many other occasions. However, it flared up with a vengeance and I collapsed the first evening and remembered nothing until the next morning. I spent the day alone in a strange house while the others were out birding.

I was taken back to Hodeidah from where I took a taxi to Abs. Once again I was so happy to be back in my little shack. I have never been off sick here, and one wonders where one would spend the sick time – in the yard? So one has no option but to carry on or return to the UK and I was never quite ill enough for that. This time I put myself on a course of antibiotics that are easily obtainable at the local pharmacy.

Another memorable bird-watching experience occurred in a wadi not far from Abs. It was late afternoon and we had stopped about a quar-ter of a mile outside a small village of round mud huts. Smoke was rising from the cooking fires for the evening meals and the small wide valley echoed with the happy sound of children playing. Herds of camel grazed amongst nearby thickets of scrubby bush while at the same time flocks of sheep and goats were being driven into their enclosures for the night by older children. Old men and women on donkeys were returning from their fields. I imagine those old women in their flowing black or white robes and conical hats to be survivors of child-rearing years or were child-less. They often look bitter and joyless, but the scene that evening was idyllic. However, I know it is far from being so. There will be people in those huts suffering chronic illnesses for whom no help is at hand.

Birds seen on these trips include various sun birds, babblers, bee-eaters, hornbills, rollers, kingfishers, and several types of brilliant starlings. Paradise flycatchers also occur here, and I have seen one in particular that had a chestnut-colored tail which it fanned out and cocked from side to side.

Security and bureaucracy Yemen style

Yemen is obsessed with security. It does not matter how many times one is 'processed' – another check is often required. The locals keep a watch-ful yet benign eye on us and if we have a visitor they soon inquire who they are and how long they will stay. A message came one day to say they did not possess records for all foreigners at the clinic, and would we present ourselves that afternoon with our passports? Accordingly, at 3:00 p.m. we washed our faces, made sure our legs were covered and went off to the *hakooma* [center of local government, police and army] which is situated on a small hill just outside the village. It is the oldest building in Abs, being an imposing jumble of an old Turkish fort and decrepit outbuildings grouped around a rough courtyard into which we drove to join a few other vehicles, groups of men, and shackled prisoners. We followed the main stream of people up a steep, filthy staircase of rock. Some of the steps were so deep I was obliged to use my hands to climb up to a crowded landing which led into a large, oblong hall or *muffrage* with colored cushions all around the wall on which sat local dignitar-ies and supplicants. Everyone looked surprised to see us, but with usual Arab courtesy we were invited in and given a place to sit after removing our shoes at the door.

In the center of one long wall sat the *Mudeer Al Nahaya* – the area supervisor – a fascinating man, wearing a long white skirt and an imposing belt and jambia. His snow-white, short-sleeved shirt showed off his beautifully shaped hands and arms – very masculine and macho. He sported a heavy gold watch and rings, his gold teeth flashed as he smiled and he held a gold pen in his hand ready to sign the many documents that were being presented to him. His splendid glossy, thick, black hair was neatly cut, he sat easily but never slovenly and he picked the odd khat leaf or twig, twirling it in his elegant fingers while exchanging pleasantries with his audience of supplicants. Some came in and squatted directly in front of him, exchanging rapid remarks. Others sitting around the room would write notes and throw them to him; these he slowly unrolled and read at the same time chatting amiably with those around him, not showing surprise or any emotion other than pleasant reasonableness. He would jot down a reply and toss it back to the person concerned. We sat quietly watching all this for twenty or thirty minutes. The great man sent a minion out to get Cokes for us which were opened with part of a Kalashnikov rifle. He inquired what had we come for, was it about the new clinic? We said 'no,' but we had heard he wanted to see us. He laughed indulgently, disclaiming knowledge of such a message, adding that it was in any case a pleasure to see us! He was the personification of power and male dominance, around thirty years old, handsome with a slightly wicked and cruel look. I was spellbound. He reminded me of a sleek well-fed tiger. After a while someone indicated we could go, which we did, backwards, almost falling over the waiting shackled prisoners.

Visit to Marharbisha

At last an opportunity to visit Marharbisha arrived and we traveled four hours east through wide wadis. One had a delightful little stream in it with mossy green banks. I resisted the temptation to paddle, and just observed this charming scene as well as a long-tailed paradise flycatcher darting in and out of tall swaying, silky grasses. From here we climbed up a steep and fearsome mountainside to arrive in the verdant shallow valley in which khat leaves are harvested from small, leafy bushes resembling tea, or slender trees that reminded me of young birch saplings. Great care is taken with the irrigated khat terraces that are so neat and tidy, in stark comparison to the town itself which is utterly filthy with muddy, pot-holed streets full of vehicles from donkey carts, ancient, decrepit old trucks to glamorous, modern estate cars, all equipped with powerful radios. These various transports all rush up and down the mountain road carrying freshly picked khat leaves to sell along the main road from Hodeidah to Saudi Arabia. Khat must be fresh. I am told it cannot be stored and is usually chewed in the afternoons before evening prayers.

More later.

Love, Mum

Eleven

1 March

Dearest Sue and Dennis,

I was thrilled, really, to get letters from all three of you last week as I especially needed them. My morale was low. They came in the nick of time in order to reassure me I have another life someplace else; that someone cares for me somewhere. I have been in Abs almost two months without a break apart from the disastrous visit to Taiz in January when I was quite ill with sinusitis.

The other midwife has been away for three weeks and I have had many calls plus the hectic morning clinic of sick children. We have been seeing forty or fifty every day, and our Yemeni staff have been away from work frequently. The new doctors (husband and wife) are around; they are good at their jobs and pleasant enough, but cool. They are an asset to the project and are picking up Arabic quickly. I'm not so anxious about my language ability anymore.

I've had twelve difficult midwifery cases in the past two weeks; five had to be sent on to the city. Almost every type of mal-presentation has turned up. Although I've been busy in this way there are still quite a few hours for me to fill each day in the yard.

Today is the day off – Friday. I felt I couldn't face another midwifery disaster so announced I would not be at home. At least I can relax today and tonight without fearing the bang on the gates. It's a good thing I like letter writing. It is a form of communication for me, because here I hardly have any communication; my Arabic hardly constitutes that. The two doctors live separately from us. When the other midwife is here she keeps to her room – she doesn't wish to have any ordinary conversation – and to counteract this I have to develop some activity. Of course, there are times when we have official visitors or a series of meetings. Our new coordinator will soon be down here. He is pretty loquacious, I think.

The climate is still reasonable but dusty. The sick children we see present mainly with chest infections, malaria, TB (rampant here) and always malnutrition and anemia. The new doctors are starting a register of TB cases which has never been done here before.

I was interested to read about your business news. It all sounds interesting and stimulating and all the more so for being one's own boss. People work better and more creatively if they do something on their own. I know I do. One of my problems here is that I seem to be bereft of ideas for the work, and if I do have any they are promptly squashed by the younger ones. But I must not blame others. Another aspect of the job is that we work in such a crazy Kafkaesque set-up, with no authority to change anything. I have never worked in such a manner before. It is about all I can do to do my own job and I can't imagine how we can improve anything as things are.

These projects are set up by idealists who believe human nature is basically good, and if not, it has been thwarted and poisoned by society! Therefore, change society. They also think you can change it by example, but I can't see Yemenis wanting to emulate us. We don't take money from people and we live poorly. We do things simply with no high-powered technology which is what they like. They just think we are mad.

A new social researcher is joining our other team – her name is Suzie.

Yes, I would love to visit you next year. I leave early May 1986 and would like to go straight to Shrewsbury to tidy up the garden and enjoy my house. I have an idea: as I've always wanted to visit New England in the fall, perhaps I could do that en route? But it's early days and there are times here when I'm just about to pick up my purse and get on the afternoon bus out of here and never come back!

I have a five-day break in Sana'a in three weeks' time. I've been too long in Abs without a break. I do try and take an objective view. After all, it's not long until my next holiday of six weeks.

I wrote the monthly statistics all in Arabic today and they look good! Took me an hour. Judy usually does them. I can't even spend money to amuse myself here. There's nothing I particularly want in Yemen, but I must get a few strange gifts sometime in Sana'a.

Love, Mum

22 April

Dearest Suzanne and Dennis,

It's 7:00 p.m. I am sitting at a table of sorts on my verandah. It was constructed by Tony last year from old planks and scraps of plywood found around the yard, which he had then covered with plastic. It is good enough for Abs. Conditions are extremely hot and sweaty but very few mosquitoes are around just now. Everything is covered with a layer of dust. This is the dust-storm time. Looking back in my diary I see that we had the same occurrence last year. I am reasonably cheerful and quite well physically. I think this climate is more healthy than Malawi. It is very dry and there are not many flies either.

Each day plods on as before. Most of the time one can't complain of overwork. Three mornings a week I work in the children's room, which is not as busy as before – although I have had to do several days without our doctor, and on one day sixty-six children came. I used to see many more than that in Bulawayo in Zimbabwe but they were not sick children and the clinic went on until 4:00 p.m. there. Judy organizes the crowd and helps me when I need moral support. The other three mornings I go visiting in the houses. You go to see one, you are then taken to several others in the neighborhood. Lots of new babies. So many women have ten or eleven pregnancies and are incredibly anemic. We've had several tenth-pregnancy twins! You wonder what nature is playing at. It's almost impossible to get the women to take iron pills or any other pills regularly. It's strange – on the whole, they are desperate to have medicine, but then don't take it.

Two afternoons a week we sweat it out at the antenatal clinic. We often get a gang of women coming together, maybe not pregnant (at least they are not aware of being so), but wanting to talk about their complaints and expecting magic cures. Women stop one on the street saying they can't get pregnant – why? and expect an answer there and then. I feel like saying, 'aren't you lucky'! I did say to one group of women that it isn't necessary for all women to have babies. They always ask why my daughters don't have children. I say that my daughters say there are lots of women willing to have babies, they prefer not to. Surprisingly, some of the older women understand this. I wish I could speak more Arabic though. I am obliged to drink all sorts of tea, coffee, and water in every house and never get sick from it.

Thanks for your letter dated 21 March. Hope all goes well for your trip to Hawaii. Sorry if I sound depressed sometimes but letter writing is the only outlet I have at those times. It passes.

Someone goes to Sana'a tomorrow and will post this letter for me. I go there in a week for four days to renew my driving license. We had a long rainstorm yesterday and the countryside is transformed today, the air sparkling and clear.

Love, Mum

Twelve

3 May

Dearest Suzanne and Dennis,

I am having three days in Sana'a after a fairly exhausting time in Abs recently. We have at least had rain, so it's not quite as hot as last year. In fact, the whole country has had heavy rain and looks wonderful.

I am enjoying my time here in Sana'a. The first evening I was my usual jibbering idiot self after traveling from Abs by group taxi for nine hours. In the evening someone suggested we go to the Sheraton – so I couldn't refuse. I bathed, pulled on a decent dress and shoes and off we went. Had a very expensive drink in the bar on top of the hotel, then a fish buffet supper. Four of us had a good laugh and enjoyed it. Yesterday I was invited to a Philippino lunch at the embassy club. It seemed just like a chicken stew with some pineapple in it, but it was good. In the evening there was a party given by Liz G, the Oxfam representative here. She left this morning for a smart wedding (hers!) in Surrey next week. They will also have another party for young friends in London, after the wedding reception for family etc. The party here wasn't too big. I knew most people: several British vets; teachers from the British Council and university; American Peace Corps workers we had known in Abs and

Hodeidah; and the Ambassador and his wife who have visited us in Abs. There was dancing, food, lots of cold beer, and most folk were in some sort of festive dress!

People are very interested in our work here – specially someone as old as I am doing it. It is good for my battered ego. I got pulled up to dance and took lots of photos. I came home at midnight exhausted!

Tomorrow I renew my driving license and do some shopping. I am invited to a teacher's flat in the university grounds for supper. I go back to Abs on Sunday with Gerry, 'our man in Sana'a.' We only have to work two weeks before we return to Sana'a for our six-monthly conference of three days. Then it is Ramadan until 20 June. On 28 June I leave for my holidays away from Yemen.

I get lots of letters and I write lots too. I find them a great pleasure. One can feel so anonymous and isolated in Abs. To get letters means you are 'someone.' There is another world outside Yemen! One does have family and friends who care for one.

Hope all is well with you.

Love, Mum

24 May

Dearest Suzanne and Dennis,

This has been a most exhausting week. We all left Abs at 10:00 a.m. Monday and drove seven hours to Sana'a with hardly any break. During Ramadan you can't have picnics or be seen drinking anything, even water, during the daytime. The valleys, mountains and wadis look quite beautiful now because there has been lots of rain for six to eight weeks. Miles and miles of terraces up sloping mountainsides are all covered with sprouting green crops that look like green moss in the distance.

Tuesday to Thursday this week we had our six-monthly conference. There are very few of us so active participation is expected by all. This is when we plan our work and decide how we will do it. We need to have these meetings – both in Abs (frequently) and in Sana'a twice a year to coordinate what we do. We talk about recruitment needs and development work generally, conditions in Yemen, what we find at the grass roots and set ourselves targets for the next few months. We are forever trying to devise ways of evaluating our work in the light of the overall objectives of our group. I am now going to write my second six-monthly report in the next few days.

Our conference finished at 1:00 p.m. today. We were invited to the British Ambassador's house for lunch. It was a great treat. They are of course charming and very interested in our work. They live in an old stone house with a huge entrance door of carved wood. The entrance hall has flowers, Persian rugs and a silver salver; the lounge has large chintz-covered chairs, heavy velvet curtains, beautiful small silver objects on coffee tables, table lamps with beautiful bases, more lovely rugs, and charming water colors on the walls (just like colonial days). Uniformed elderly attendants brought us drinks on silver trays. Everything was very quiet, refined and dignified. The lunch table was set as in the old days: plates with crest that must be in the right place. It was at least a buffet. We had lots of wine. I thoroughly enjoyed the decent meal – I can't remember when I last had one. Of course there's a walled garden with water sprinklers on, looking very green. The Ambassador's wife is always asking us to call on her anytime we are around. I might do that one day!

Love, Mum

Diary entry: Feeling isolated and a bit hopeless before my break

It is almost time for me to go on holiday again, and I am not popular because the Ministry of Health want us to be ready with ten ladies prepared to take a month-long course in family welfare quite soon. Originally, this was to have been a refresher course for the established, traditional birth attendants but they adamantly refused to join, in spite of the promise of thousands of rials to be provided by central and local government and ourselves. To 'go to a school' would indicate they did not know everything. But by now we know several older ladies, widowed or unmarried, who are interested but illiterate. A lot of work has to be done while I am away, arranging accommodation for the Sudanese health visitor who will conduct the course, getting agreements drawn up for the ladies, the local authorities and the Ministry in Sana'a.

At this moment I am suffocating in my room under the fan which blows hot air on me. But outside a big storm is brewing, the air is thick with dust, and the sky and landscape in one direction are enveloped in a black curtain that sweeps across the desolate scrub. We hope rain will come in our direction but it often only threatens with cracks of thunder. Outside our yard, on the dirt track and through the rubbish dumps, small noisy motorbikes rush up and down incessantly. They supplement the local taxis on souk days, often carrying three people, or two and a sheep. Even in the narrow alleys of the souk they pursue one. Yesterday afternoon Tony and I went up the wadi by car. He thought we might see some birds, but no, the black atmosphere was eerily silent and still – even the birds were hiding.

I returned from this outing at 7:00 p.m. feeling profoundly listless and inexpressibly tired. I could hardly summon the energy to put up my net and organize my bedding. The last six months have not been among the best in my life; intermittent stomach problems, incipient sinusitis, the language difficulty and then a dog bite from one of the mangy creatures that live on the rubbish dumps have all had a debilitating effect on me. I hasten to add that I received a course of anti-rabies and antibiotic injections for the bite which was not a deep wound; my long dress prevented the fangs penetrating deeply. In spite of all these difficulties I still hope to stay for the two years and three months agreed to. I must also add that I can be restored quite swiftly to a cheerful frame of mind. Just to wake up on a cool early morning to a bright clear sky before sun-up, to hear and see the flocks of bee-eaters whirling and warbling overhead, to watch the yellow weavers picking seeds from my sorghum plants only three feet from my bed – all this is enough to restore me to a normal frame of mind for a while longer.

Thirteen

Letter and diary extracts

I felt very sad leaving Katherine and all my dear friends and neighbors when I returned to Yemen last week. Katherine saw me to the airport, where I discovered I should have checked my booking three days before.

I was therefore put on 'stand by.' Katherine and I had a decent lunch. She then left the airport. I had to wait until twenty minutes before take-off to find out if I was on the flight. Nerve-wracking, but I got a seat which turned out to be in first class all the way to Sana'a! We traveled by Air Bus to Cairo, where I had a seven-hour wait for a 707 (the aircraft's name was *Tutankamen*) to Sana'a. I took a taxi into town. I felt unhappy and exhausted that first day, but slept well that night and felt just fine the next day and determined to enjoy my last few months in Yemen. I also decided, as part of the positive approach, to take seven to ten days off at Christmas and go to Damascus and Amman. I shall make definite arrangements in October.

After two days in Sana'a I found out that down in Hodeidah a big palaver was going on amongst the taxi people. At last I was pushed, unceremoniously together with six men, into the back of a large van-type conveyance. There were at least fifteen other passengers, arranged like sardines, but the front seat was occupied by an Arab lady and her children. An Arab woman cannot risk being touched by a man other than her husband. At Abs I was released from my cramped position in the taxi onto the main road; I picked my way through the rubbish dump, by the disconsolate discarded donkeys and the mangy dogs, to our yard to find all had changed here apart from my room. It is quite amazing to find myself back in this desolate environment.

While I was away, Judy and others have been stressfully employed setting up the month-long school for older women. In order to give the teacher relatively comfortable lodgings for that month, Judy has moved out to a house nearby and I am to share the compound with the Sudanese trainer, Limandaamat, who will also use our office as her lecture room. Fortunately I get along well with her and she was happy that I was not thinking of moving out in spite of the lack of privacy. I have things in common with her that I do not have with my young colleagues, such as being much older and having experienced nursing in colonial Africa. Her nursing qualifications (SRN, SCN and HV) were obtained through that system and she had nothing but praise for it. [These were UK nursing qualifications: State Registered Nurse (SRN), State Certified Nurse (SCN) and Health Visitor (HV).] It had given her a profession, independence and the ability to support her family in her own country and elsewhere. Being a Christian in a mainly Muslim land had not always been easy for her. She is a large, comfortable lady who exudes authority and confidence. I felt exhausted one day after night calls, and she had massaged my feet; I found it so soothing, not just because of the massage but for the compassion shown and companionship offered.

The ladies who come to the classes are incredibly enthusiastic and adore their teacher, each pupil vying for favor by giving gifts or doing housework. Some of the things they are taught are quite irrelevant to life in Abs! I sat in on a demonstration of baby-bathing. It was hilarious to see these tough, rough, old women bathing a baby doll western style, with a tray of all sorts of bits and pieces unobtainable in Abs, plus nappies, several clean towels, cloths for the baby, a baby bath, sterile eye swabs, sterile water etc, etc. We feel that this European-based training should be modified in order to reflect local conditions.

Two pupils feel they are superior, being from a mountain region, and wear the long black robes and cover their faces. I get the impression they have learned certain mannerisms from television 'soaps' from India. The bolder of the pair, while fluttering her mascaraed eyelashes, clutches her yashmak nervously in an exquisitely manicured hand in the approved Bollywood style in order to create the impression of sweet and desirable innocence. They live in a trading compound beside the *hakooma*. They are familiar with the personnel there and live in more sophisticated rooms than the rest of the class. This, of course, leads to all sorts of allegations, insinuations and eruptions in the classrooms. I am told these ladies have 'tongues of snakes.' On accepting an invitation from them to visit I was conducted up carpeted stairs to a large, softly lit upper room. I was taken aback at its opulent and seductive air. There were no windows that I could see but an efficient air-conditioner was in action, the walls were lined with cabinets full of beautiful clothes and literally hundreds of perfumes from which I was invited to spray myself.

During my village visits I called on my old friend Roumia, one of the long-established traditional birth attendants, to deliver a pretty plate for her wall from my home in Shrewsbury. She made a great fuss of me, and killed the 'fatted calf,' so to speak, and neighbors crowded in to share in the feast while hoping for magic cures for various chronic ailments from either Roumia or myself.

Otherwise the day-to-day activities went ahead as before except that I went into the children's room for a few weeks while the doctor was away. It is now hectic, each child accompanied by several adults who crowd around one. I am reminded of '...the hosts of Midian, how they prowl and prowl around.' I was incredibly cheered when Judy, who had been exercising crowd control in the room, paid me a compliment by saying she thought I had managed wonderfully these last few weeks during the doctor's absence. She said she was proud of me. But now she is about to

leave and pressure is being put on us to find ten young women, prefera-
bly literate, for the year's training course as supervisors of the older ones
recently given the month's course, at least that is the theory. For each of
these young women we have to produce a form of consent signed by a
male family member or village elders.

In connection with this, an unannounced deputation of six people
from the Ministry of Health arrived at eight o'clock one evening for
whom food and accommodation had to be found. That was not difficult in this hospitable society. Another great event in the village was
the examination of the ladies after their month of training – which was
something of a landmark in Yemeni village society – and the Minister
of Health made a big party out of it. She arrived the evening before
the exam with a party of ten from India, Pakistan, America, Sudan and
Yemen, most of them holding senior positions in community health in
their own countries or being officials from WHO.

Early the next morning Judy and I rushed around the village and out-
lying areas to make sure the pupils arrived on time. None of them had
ever been in such a situation. They knew nothing about exams although
their teacher had explained it all to them. It was hard for them to grasp
the importance of arriving on time. But they loved it all. It made them
feel important and they had been promised 1000 rials if they succeeded,
half of which was to be paid by the local government.

Back in the yard, the lecture room had been transformed by the
pupils under the direction of Limandaamat to resemble the practical
lecture room of circa 1939 – when I had started nursing! Our office had
never been so clean. The ladies arrived in their best dresses but quickly
huddled together in a corner, abashed and uncomprehending at the
sight of these important foreigners rushing around the sandy yard con-
sulting each other and making notes. Then Abdul Karim, the regional
Minister of Health, swept up to the yard with an armed escort. At this
point Judy and I joined the ladies in their huddle to steady all our nerves.
Later we had to go out and collect the take-away dinners we had ordered
earlier from a local cafe for the guests. Meanwhile, each pupil was given

an oral and practical test of ten to fifteen minutes each by different examiners. I was amazed at the ease with which they answered and performed. Limandaamat, being an old-fashioned person, had taught them by rote. She had captured their loyalty and devotion and they would do anything for her. Of course, they all passed and the officials pronounced the course to have been unique and utterly successful.

The next event was a prize giving for these ladies at the provincial capital of Hajja. Two had been prevented from coming by their husbands but for the others I had, once again, to run around early to get them all in the cars for the three-hour drive up the mountains. Some of them had never been so far from Abs before and they were yet again awestruck. Once there, we had to hang around not quite knowing what to expect. We found seats in a large hall, listened to interminable speeches before the prize giving – which was marred by the absence of prizes. There should have been at least certificates and midwifery bags but none of these things were ready. More importantly there was no sign of the local government's part of their payment. We have searched for the responsible gentlemen but hardly ever find them. If we do, they claim to know nothing about it or that they will soon be out of office and no longer have authority over money.

Back in Hajja, lunchtime had arrived – a grand lunch had been provided for VIPs to which our coordinator and I were invited, but nothing was offered to our ladies the prizewinners! We were shocked and refused to join the hoi polloi [in the sense of the elite]. Eventually Abdul Karim himself ordered the hospital kitchen to give us all food and it was quite good. We ate it, picnic-style, under a tree outside. That is just the bare outline of what actually occurred. I was also feeling unwell all the time with my usual complaints but was obliged to stay on in Hajja for what is euphemistically called a 'workshop' on community health. 'Workshop' is the in-word for those on the international health circuit, jetting around the world, staying in the best hotels where possible. I was curious to see if anything unique occurred at a Yemeni workshop! But no, just interminable speeches by top dogs, and no participation by those in the field.

However, not all is gloom and doom. My new, fine-mesh mosquito net from South Africa keeps out the tiny flies that attacked me most horribly last June; the bee-eaters are back, wheeling and yodeling every early morning; and my new friend Limandaamat took me, via Hajja, to her home in Rowdha for a weekend – insisting on paying all my fares and food.

Hajja is a squalid town magnificently situated on a series of craggy mountain tops, often swathed in mist. Like other towns I have mentioned, the colored-glass windows of houses that cling to the steep hillsides on the zig-zagging roads make pretty pictures resembling necklaces at night. Here, we stayed with one of the Sudanese families, who, like many expatriate groups, get together whenever they can. Today they had a traditional biscuit-making session. A large mound of flour, some salt and grated cinnamon were mixed up on a large tray to which was added what looked like melted butter. But it was butter and yoghurt boiled together until clear, and added to the flour mixture when cool. Four ladies helped to knead the dough, which was then rolled and cut up in small pieces; after cooking each piece was rolled in icing sugar – delicious!

We went on to Rowdha where most houses are of the tall, decorated, traditional type and it is now a fashionable place to live. The windows of the thick-walled house in which I stayed were of alabaster and colored glass above, with more functional windows below, from which one looked down onto mud-walled vineyards and apricot orchards. It was a charming interlude.

In September our electricity supply was cut off in Abs. We discovered that our bills had not been paid, so Judy and I paid an intriguing visit to the electricity office which is a shack out in the sandy wastes full of chaps lying about chewing khat and looking extremely relaxed. One would hardly think it was an office. Fortunately Judy's Arabic was good enough to explain the situation. We paid our bill to one of the reclining fellows who put the money into his pocket, gave us a receipt and sent a minion in a truck to climb an electricity pole near our house to 'turn it on again' but no one had seen it being turned off!

In early October Judy left, her term of service having expired. She offered to stay on as she thought I would find the mounting pressure and pace too much, but I asked her to please leave me on my own as a midwife –the other team members were around but were not involved in midwifery. Her replacement would arrive in three months. In any case, by now our part of the project was well in hand. It had a momentum of its own. The Ministry of Health was determined to set up the next training session. Because we were unable to find literate ladies ready and willing to take this course, the group decided that we should go ahead and recruit women who were keenly interested and free from utter male domination! After all, being an illiterate female in this society does not mean she is not clever or intelligent. We had been amazed by the speed and ease with which the older women had learned by rote and from practical demonstration. By now these ladies were feeling somewhat disconsolate because the local government authority showed no inclination to pay them the promised 500 rials. In addition they were not called upon immediately by the village people who still preferred the tried and tested midwives who had been watching this experiment with tolerant amusement, secure in their well-established positions. Judy and I visited them frequently to keep them informed, treating them as superior colleagues, which they were. But at least our ladies knew something helpful to their families and friends. They brought crowds of children for immunizations, women for antenatal care and accompanied us on our home visits, translating our health messages.

We received many random messages from Sana'a saying or threatening that the new Sudanese trainer would arrive any moment. Are you ready? We were not quite sure what 'being ready' involved. This course is for a year; consent forms have to be signed by a guardian, a proper classroom and equipment are needed, and accommodation must be found for the tutor. We dashed up to Marharbisha one day to visit and meet the tutor and find out what she required. Everything seemed to be up in the air and we are never sure the course will really get under way. There are crates of new classroom equipment from UNICEF in the new unfinished clinic building but we are forbidden to open them. I visited Sana'a for a conference and to see the Ministry of Health regarding the course and to collect the certificates for the older ladies. I had to fill them out myself and search for an appropriate person to sign them.

Arriving back in Abs after nightfall to an empty, dusty, desolate yard, suffering with an upset stomach, I found a huge scorpion scurrying around the small dust-encrusted latrine – called the *hamaan* here. After some dancing around I managed to kill it and cover the body with an upturned bucket on which I put a large stone to make quite sure it couldn't resurrect itself! The next pleasant surprise was that the water tank, polluted by a rotting lizard, had to be emptied and cleaned out before more water could be ordered the following morning.

Fiona, on a visit from the UK, came down for three days and I was pleased to be able to take her across the desert to talk to some literate girls about the course. After being well feasted we were then lectured, politely, by the village headman on the evils of western ways and of encouraging young women to leave families for even a few hours each day for the course. Being in the clinic and putting them at risk of seeing men's bodies or of their faces being seen by men would make them worthless as brides.

Again Judy and I went to a village about twenty miles north from here where we met sheikhs and schoolteachers in our efforts to find literate girls. We were fed savory rice, meat and a dish called *lafuut* which is a spongy bread soaked in sour milk and onions over which local honey, a great luxury, is poured. All this was followed by local grapes and illegally imported oranges.

On another recruiting trip we got the response: yes, the girls can be trained but only if the instruction is given in their homes! In any case, there would always be the problem of transporting them plus a guardian, into Abs every day. In the end we settled for ten women from Abs who could be signed up and vouched for. Then their documents were scrutinized in Sana'a. The Ministry of Health implied obliquely that it was our fault they were illiterate! But by now we had developed thick skins. As long as we had ten eager ladies, the course would begin and we looked after these ten like a hen with chicks. Even so, every day some minor calamity seemed to threaten our plans. We cannot be sure they will not change their minds or that the local government authority will come up with their part of the payment. They still have not paid the older ladies.

Bird-watching trips provided welcome relief from this nail-biting exercise. One trip took us to the coast through picturesque, pure-desert scenery interspersed with patches of brilliant green sorghum where wells have been sunk. On the way, we passed the salt hills of Jabal al-Milh and, on the horizon, the famous, much-painted outlines of the al-Mu'tarid mosque and fort – the huge edifice of the latter appears to be declining slowly into the sand. At the wild, unspoiled beach, the clear blue sea, flocks of flamingoes and smaller waders, a few osprey, pelicans, heron and ibis were a joy to behold. Another day, in Wadi Surdud, where we were able to park under trees, we had no need to search for amethyst starlings with their salmon-pink back patches, white fronts and iridescent heads and tail feathers. Abyssinian rollers, showing off their exquisite bright-turquoise plumage with a darker blue stripe on the wings and reddy brown neck patches, sat singing on the tops of trees; tiny sunbirds darted in and out of furry nests delicately suspended from twigs. We heard the plaintive call of bee-eaters that live in burrows on the dried river bank and observed several Abdims storks, flocks of Arabian sparrows and silverbills splashing in a small pool.

Because we have been so busy with the recruiting saga plus several horrid midwifery complications and I am so often unwell, it has been decided I should have a few days off in the lull before the storm that will accompany the opening of the school. I chose to visit Don and Mary who are my ideal volunteer workers. They are cheerful, efficient, have integrated well with the local population and have some previous experience in the Arab world. Within the group it had been decided they should live in a mountain village to help and encourage health workers already trained to commence mobile immunization caravans that will go to remote areas far from any form of health care.

I met the usually immaculate Don and Mary at Bayt al Faqir look-ing tired and disheveled. They had been in a remote mountain village for several days, staying in unfinished buildings with no sanitary facili-ties. They are in the process of opening and equipping six village health rooms and then supervising the work. This means being out walking in the mountains for four days a week using a donkey for carrying equip-ment and then returning to base to clean up, write reports, etc. Our two-hour journey to their village involved crossing irrigated desert to reach the mouth of a narrow wadi where we joined an extremely steep and rocky track and passed thick patches of bush, banana groves, mango and custard apple trees. Their village – a collection of small houses, shops, a mosque and a school – has been built on the side of a ravine.

They occupy a charming terraced house with a little balcony over-looking the ravine and on which potted plants are flourishing, meals are eaten, washing-up is done. The water from that task is then used for irrigation. They have a constant stream of visitors to discuss the next journey's logistics, refrigeration of vaccines and any other health mat-ters. There is no doctor nearby so they are much in demand but are not openly involved in midwifery as we are in Abs.

I had hoped to go on safari with them but didn't feel equal to the rig-ors involved. I simply rested for two days before returning to Bayt al Faqir to get a bus on to Taiz where I socialized with American acquaintances and their Yemeni friends and with whom I visited a khat-growing region in the mountains south of Taiz. The souks here are run by women from a tribe famed for their Amazonian characteristics and we were fascinated to see these powerful, handsome ladies conducting business from their small Toyota trucks while their armed menfolk squatted in groups chat-ting, smoking and chewing while keeping sharp eyes on the business.

The weather was quite wintery in Sana'a where I again visited the Minister of Health about the training course. She shouted, threateningly, that we must be ready by 15 January. Fortunately our new midwife is here, a soothing, unflappable, capable girl. She gave me courage to return to Abs where I found the children's room to be almost unmanageable.

The doctor looks tired and ill but I can do nothing to help. There are two doctors in our group plus the government doctor. They should be able to work something out between them. At least it is much cooler in Abs, and I go visiting every day with one of the ladies from the previous course or my counterpart, Fatima, who would love to pamper me as she did Limandaamat.

Fatima and I spend some time together improving my Arabic and she learns a few English words, which she is thrilled about. She took me to visit her brother's family for a picnic in a pretty, peaceful wadi where they grow tomatoes. We came away loaded. A lady friend who comes to Fatima's house on a donkey brings sour milk for me in gourds that hang from her saddle. Fatima keeps it in her fridge – along with Coke and cold water for me – and I wonder if that narrow-necked gourd is ever cleaned, but that doesn't prevent me from enjoying it.

There are many night calls. I took the visiting Oxfam representative around the village together with Fatima to show what we are about. There was a huge party in our yard which passed before my eyes like a film. Joan, our doctor did all the work. The cool weather brought a crop of visitors getting to know the country, and I finished writing my six-monthly report.

Then one day the promised teacher called in to see the apartments chosen for her by the local government authority by reason of their cheapness. She was not happy with them and won't come here unless something better is offered. In desperation we have offered to give up one of our dwellings which seems to suit both her and the local government who can now wriggle out of paying rent on her behalf.

Unannounced, the regional Minister of Heath swept in with his armed entourage to open the new clinic building. We were not involved in this activity but observed from a distance. The clinic staff strung tape across the yard for him to cut and announce the clinic open but we are still forbidden to open the UNICEF crates of equipment needed for the new midwifery school. When the great ones had gone, the locals entered into games and contests on the desolate football field. They were nourished by sunflower seeds and Coke. I am reminded of the 'bread and circus' of a Roman feast, but without the feast, and for 'feast' read 'khat.'

Our antenatal clinic continues more or less as a social meeting but most of the ladies are pregnant anyway. Those who are not come to find out why they are not. During one of these sessions a cavalcade of trucks swept into the clinic yard carrying at least six gory bodies of men wounded by gunshot at the border army checkpoint while trying to smuggle through a box of oranges. As the afternoon somnolence was shattered by this violent noise and scene, our ladies scattered, screaming, their pretty, flimsy robes flying behind them. One or two of them although pregnant, managed to climb through the back window. One exclaimed she would faint unless we gave her a pill, any pill! So we produced a folic acid pill which worked wonders and gave her the strength to exit through the back window. Crowds of locals poured into the yard hoping to see something of this sinister event, but the victims were soon taken off to Hodeidah, leaving only a trail of blood on the ground and a smell of diesel and scorched tires in the air. I am sorry to say that one of them was already dead on arrival with pockets stuffed with oranges...

That night I had three calls into the village. While walking from one house to another followed by family groups, I met the Sudanese doctor who had also been called out. I appreciated the feeling of camaraderie and wished we could have worked more closely with him.

Christmas Day

In spite of everything this has been one of the most enjoyable Christmas Days of my life and certainly the most unique. We worked as usual, but in the evening Joan prepared a tasty vegetarian dish, I provided a Christmas pudding with sherry sauce, put candles inside tall Nescafe jars and listened to King's College Boys Choir while eating. Immediately after, I was called out and on my way back at 1:00 a.m., wandering with one of my friends through the narrow alleyways under a full moon to the sound of animals chewing and rustling in the yards, I seemed to be part of a biblical scene and felt really happy and elated.

I haven't yet told you of how a flourishing shopping area has sprung up around the entrance to our yard where only a year ago was waste land. Now one can get a hot meal, watch TV, buy milk, tobacco, petrol, paraffin, etc. My friend and I dropped in for a Coke at 2:00 a.m. So endeth my best Christmas Day.

A day or two later a few of us paid a visit to a rugged, far-distant mountain area north of Abs where I am sure no European woman has been before. Our meeting place with local government officials was in a fortified house, built in loose stone on a craggy rock. Our arrival must have been observed, for, as we came near this storied building, we could see that from every window lolled a white-clad, turbaned figure chewing khat, the whole scene resembling a house of rag dolls. The interior was dark, cavernous and full of people coming and going. We were conducted to the top room from where we had the most splendid views over a wide green plain towards Marharbisha in the east and over wide desert land towards the sea in the west.

While we were away, Joan had fabricated a method by which lizards could be prevented from getting into our water tank – resourceful girl. The following day I took the bus to Hodeidah for three days. By now the drivers know me and this is pleasant as I no longer feel like a total alien. Like all others workers who have survived the two years and are in an on-going assignment, I was asked if I would consider staying on for a further two years. I wish I could. I wish I were tough enough, but I am not.

In Hodeidah I finished typing my six-monthly report, took a walk on the beach, avoiding dead cats and other unrecognizable filth, to enjoy a glorious sunset. Took a taxi back. The driver was very civil and charming and he took me right up to our door. On New Year's Day I awoke early feeling marvelously well and cheerful – perhaps because Ann, the new midwife, will soon be here to share the problems we will face getting this started or to face the awful disappointment if, for some reason or another, it does not start. All will be revealed in my next letter.

Fourteen

THE FINAL FEW MONTHS: JANUARY–APRIL 1986

After Christmas Jean had a few weeks time off to visit her home and family in the UK. She resumes her story with her return to Sana'a in the New Year.

Letter and diary extracts

Before leaving Yemen I must complete the story for you as far as I am concerned. Returning from the UK in January the weather was blissfully cool but horribly dusty. This resulted in a great increase in children's chest complaints followed by a measles epidemic during which two young children from the same family died within twenty-four hours. I continued with the midwifery calls which are as nothing compared to the calls I would get in Malawi, but the situations cannot be compared. There I worked in a reasonably equipped hospital with a doctor available. But whereas I am not able to remember any particularly gruesome case from Malawi – because there were so many – I am able to recall one here.

The lady came in with strong contractions, the baby already dead presenting a shoulder and chest. What was I to do? No doctor, no anesthetic, only my soulmate Ayesha to help me plus a horde of relatives providing the chorus. No one wanted her to go to Hodeidah. Ayesha, no doubt in the pay of the relatives, slapped me on the back saying, 'Come on Jean, we can do it'! Had I not been there I am sure she would have had a go herself. The patient and family were extremely cooperative and I'm pleased to say I managed to deliver the child as a breech, without further harm to the mother. It was one of those stressful moments in midwifery when you wish you had never taken up this work. But then, one is flooded with relief and thankfulness for the results, as were the relatives and the patient herself. On occasions I have been amazed at the truly touching scenes of affection and sympathy shown by husbands to their wives when they stay for the delivery, but few do. It is very much a woman's world.

Ann and James arrived to stay in early January. Ann is the new midwife and she is a delight, so fresh and cheerful, tackling problems with sense and good humor. The village ladies were also charmed by her, taking her along to their social functions. She must have found it a strain but gave no sign of it. For me it was good to have a companion for the evening meal and we vied with each other as to who could produce the tastiest dish, mainly thick soups and yoghurt and fruity puddings with honey.

Soon after Ann's arrival we made another trip to Marharbisha to establish friendly contact with the new teacher. We wanted her to feel needed and cared for. We again passed through the wide green wadi with its sparkling stream, flower-strewn banks flanked by swaying, feathery canes and tall grasses. It was idyllic, made more so by the stark contrast with the surrounding landscape. We went on up the rough, rocky, car-wreckage-strewn road to Marharbisha, meeting the crazy convoys of khat-laden Toyota trucks rushing down towards Abs and the main road in time for the afternoon 'chew.'

Meanwhile Ann and I attend the midwifery calls, antenatal clinics and visit the ladies who trained last year. They are disappointed in not getting immediate lucrative business, but at last they did receive the 500 rials from the local government office and we support them with friendship and encouragement to bring children to the clinic for immunizations, and pregnant ladies for check-ups. We keep in constant touch with the provincial HQ (PHQ) trying to ascertain when we can expect the teacher. We don't want her to be discouraged by finding no house ready. I was anxious all the time that the course might collapse for reasons beyond our control, such as no money in local government coffers or that transport arrangements for the two girls living outside Abs will not materialize. Then, a week later, the teacher arrived, unannounced, hoping to start the school on 3 February. I just cannot describe to you all the intrigue and double-dealing that has been going on between the rival factions, i.e. local, provincial, central government and ourselves. There have been endless meetings during which we have been insulted, accused, etc.

Ann and I chased around the country bringing in all the girls for a meeting with local officials only for them to be told they would get no money or transport! If they wanted training they must do it for love of country! We threatened to leave and sent for our coordinator from Sana'a. All was quiet for two days and then there was a big pow-wow at the *hakooma* with all the warring factions. At this point I retired from the procession of meetings, feeling ill with all the uncertainty. You cannot imagine the obstacles there have been, and still are, the root cause being that the present members of local government do not want to stand by the agreement made by their predecessors when the project started. Fortunately, we have an anthropologist on our team who has studied Yemeni society and speaks good Arabic. He attends the meetings and joins their khat chews, doing business while socializing. At their last meeting all was sweetness, light and feasting. The girls will be paid, transport will be provided, we can use the as-yet-unfinished clinic (another saga here), we may open the UNICEF crates of equipment for the classroom – under supervision – and the teacher can have a decent house to live in. Meanwhile she has gone to Sana'a for a few days. We hope to see a driver with transport for the girls not in the village; we hope to see the guard who will supervise the opening of the crates; and we hope the teacher will return on time for the school opening on Monday and that she has not been scared off!

Another problem we had at this time was with two women we know well who wanted to join this new course; they had already taken last year's course and had been highly unpopular with the other women. I've mentioned them before. They keep a restaurant-cum-hotel near the *hakooma* and feel themselves to be a cut above the local women. They have not been refused the course to their faces, but the teacher, who is well aware of local sentiment, sends them over to the *mudeer* who then sends them to us. We have no power to say they can take the course, or perhaps we do but do not want to wreck the whole thing. The feeling against them locally is too great for us to ignore. The two women in question seem to have plenty of money and freedom to go around local, provincial and central government to lodge their protests. They come to our door frequently, draped in black, sometimes accusing me of preventing their admission. The outcome, like a lot of things that seem irresolvable, eventually fizzled out. They didn't join the class and no doubt lots of resentment will be stored up in their minds.

The most memorable event in these turbulent days and indeed in the whole of my time there was the opening of the UNICEF crates of classroom equipment. A message was received by the *mudeer* that supervisors from PHQ would come that day to open the crates. They arrived as well-armed soldiers who formed a circle around us as we toiled away unpacking all sorts of equipment never before seen in Abs, which included brilliant posters for teaching anatomy and a skeleton which caused quite a stir. The teacher and her pupils had a great time fitting out their lecture room. When I entered it the next day I was literally struck dumb and I almost cried, for, 'it had come to pass....' It was so orderly, so reminiscent of the nursing lecture rooms of my youth and such a stark contrast to the seeming chaos outside. Several moments passed before the happy realization dawned on me that the course would actually begin.

During all this current activity we had a German midwife staying. She was doing her country tour, as we all had done initially, and hoped to start a similar project at Wadi Mawr. It was highly satisfying to have had such a hectic and positive picture to present to her. Although the school started on 11 February, we have only seven pupils. We need three more to satisfy the Ministry of Health, so our capable teacher has now taken over the recruiting in the company of several students.

During all this activity we were visited by a Foreign Office minister from London and the Ambassador from Sana'a. Local dignitaries came in with half a roast lamb. After the VIPs had departed the women came along with a dish of *Bint a Sahn,* a delicious concoction of light pastry and honey, too late for the visitors, but we were not sorry. One of the outcomes of this visit was that the Embassy indicated they would support a modest literacy course for women in Abs. We had an adequate teacher on the spot in the person of our clinic clerk, a young woman of charm and dignified bearing. Her father had been an imam and had instructed her in Arab literature and the Koran.

Before the lessons started Ann and I took four of our students to Hodeidah one afternoon to see the women's literacy program there. We were amazed to find that about 700 women attend afternoon classes in crowded, hot rooms, studying – at various levels – writing, maths, sewing and typing. Back in the town the girls wanted to go off on their own to the gold souk to exchange their dowry gold for another design. Apparently this is common practice, but then at the arranged departure time there was no sign of our girls. As time went by I became extremely anxious. I imagined them having been abducted, lost forever and what would happen back at Abs? But Ann had a more relaxed attitude, calming my worst fears, and of course the girls turned up an hour late full of excitement and chatter, each blaming the other for being late. We returned to Abs in good humor to find our team members about to set up a search party.

We have our usual day off on Fridays but that doesn't stop the hammering on the door. After such a day of ten calls we decided, for our next day off, to take a trip to Al Luhaya, a decaying seaside town of former glory. Some walls and doorways still standing have exquisite carvings on them. It remains a busy fishing port for small boats, but because of its inaccessibility to inland markets the fish is smoked in beehive-shaped mud ovens situated on the shores of a lagoon. It is a picturesque sight, with colored boats at anchor on a narrow strip of water behind which grow tall bright-green grasses. I found Al Luhaya charming and worthy of another visit. On our way there we passed through the irrigated desert areas. In one place the landscape changed on account of salt mounds pushing their way through the sand making corrugated hills. Salt has been harvested here for centuries and still is. It is crushed by hand and sent out in palm-frond sacks on camel-back. I am beginning to be charmed by this desert landscape with its fantastic old forts and houses sticking up like cardboard cut-outs against the sky, its patches of emerald-green crops amidst the golden sandy expanses, the frequent tube-wells gushing water, camel herds browsing among the few areas of thorny scrub, flocks of sheep tended by cheerful, ragged children, strings of laden donkeys ridden by old women wearing the long black or orange gown and the tall, conical, Tihama straw hats.

While we were away the Minister of Health from Sana'a had paid a visit, expecting to be taken around by one of the midwives. She was briefed by other team members who were relaxing in the compound for their 'day off' and this made us feel extremely guilty.

After the opening of the school I went to Sana'a for a few days R & R: a euphemism – there is no R & R in our bleak transit house. I felt so unwell and suffered several horrible hours of black depression such as I have never before experienced. This frightened me so much that I decided immediately to return home to the UK a month earlier than scheduled in early April rather than in May when the two years and three months would have been completed.

As usual I was happy to return to Abs to write my final report, spend time in the classroom, visit the older ladies and take my turn on midwifery calls. Ann and I made a poster for the clinic walls and I am thrilled with it. We made the colored sketches and asked one of the Sudanese doctors to write a simple message in elegant Arabic script. We could have written it ourselves but it would have been so obviously the work of a foreigner!

Now that the school problems are more or less resolved, our regular meetings concentrate on the under-fives clinic and the huge work load carried by our doctor. We seem to be at an impasse – and something will have to change. I expect the resolution will come through the students, who already spend time in the clinic as part of their training, taking on more and more responsibilities; also, a new young doctor arrived with fresh practical ideas.

Before leaving Abs finally, my colleagues gave me a much-coveted book on the Tihama, illustrated with water colors and sketches. I went around the village saying, '*Masalaama*-Bye-Bye' but in every house someone was ill and I had no cure or help for them. On the day of my departure I visited the classroom and was able to make a very short speech of encouragement and thanks to the girls for not giving up the course when they were so badly treated by local officials.

In Sana'a several days passed before I could relax and enjoy my freedom! My time was spent getting exit visas, seeing friends, finishing my last report and listening to conversations in the busy transit house on the evils of western imperialism. I had two relaxed saunters in the souk buying trinkets. Investigating hitherto unexplored alleys brought me to the old coffee exchange, an impressive arched courtyard resembling the interior of a mosque. A huge weighing scale in the shape of a metal plate, at least six feet across, was suspended from the lofty roof. The only person there, apart from myself, was a ragged character sleeping on a pile of stuffed gunny sacks. The silence and passivity in this cavernous structure was more dramatic than the teeming scenes a few yards away, and, as I stood gazing at this fabled and historic place, I felt myself to be as insignificant as an ant.

A two-year ambition was realized when I visited the site of the seventh-century BC Sabean city of Marib. We traveled three hours to the east of Sana'a through red rocky, barren mountains to a black lava-covered desert to find the Marib area busy with heavy vehicles engaged in oil exploration and the reconstruction of the ancient dam. The remains of its amazing irrigation systems are still to be seen, as are some temple ruins. Rows of classical columns stand forlornly in the desert, starkly against the blue sky and little boys shin up and down between them bracing their feet and backs between the thirty-foot-high columns. The old town itself is more or less deserted. While wandering among the ruins one notices large stone blocks, engraved with ancient script, that have been used for repair work.

My final departure date, as in all things in Yemen, depends on the inscrutable Will of Allah and He sought fit to have George Bush in town the day before. The city was thick with security police, but I was fortunate in being delayed only a few hours. If I had some regrets on leaving Yemen it was over the realization that I would never see the village ladies again, specially my counterpart Fatima. I am grateful that I was a part of this project to bring some better health prospects and resources to the women and children of Yemen. The experience certainly increased my own self-knowledge.

Jean Mondon

Epilogue
After Yemen

After Jean left Yemen she was in poor health and it took a year or two for her to recover her strength again. The poor nutrition, intestinal parasites and other health concerns kept her at home in Shrewsbury in the British Midlands as she recovered.

Not to be grounded for too long, however, she arranged to go back to Africa in order to climb Mt Kilimanjaro in Tanzania when she was 68. This had been a lifelong ambition for her. Throughout my childhood I remember my mother talking about this dream of climbing the mountain. It seemed to be the one big thing she had yet to accomplish in her life. She traveled solo and hired a Tanzanian porter and guide to accompany her on her trek. I am happy to report that she made it! A photo of Jean at the snowy summit for Mt Kilimanjaro hung on the wall of her room for years afterwards and we referred to it often if she was having a hard day, to inspire her to keep going. Jean lived to the age of 90. I am fortunate to have had her as my mother. She has inspired me in my own life and was a true model of the strong women we all aspire to be. Thank you Jean! Your story lives on – it deserved to be told after all.

Suzanne Elliott (Mondon)

www.ingramcontent.com/pod-product-compliance
Lightning Source LLC
Chambersburg PA
CBHW070736250726
48662CB00004B/1562